You Learn by Living

Books by Eleanor Roosevelt

Hunting Big Game in the Eighties:
The Letters of Elliott Roosevelt, Sportsman

When You Grow Up to Vote

It's Up to the Women

A Trip to Washington with Bobby and Betty

This Is My Story

My Days

The Lady of the White House

This Troubled World

Christmas: A Story

Christmas 1940

The Moral Basis of Democracy

This Is America

If You Ask Me

This I Remember

Partners: The United Nations and Youth

India and the Awakening East

UN: Today and Tomorrow

It Seems to Me

Ladies of Courage

United Nations: What You Should Know about It

On My Own

Growing Toward Peace

You Learn by Living

The Autobiography of Eleanor Roosevelt

Your Teens and Mine

Eleanor Roosevelt's Book of Common Sense Etiquette
(with the assistance of Robert O. Ballou)

Eleanor Roosevelt's Christmas Book

Tomorrow Is Now

You Learn by Living

*Eleven Keys for a
More Fulfilling Life*

Eleanor Roosevelt

FIRST HARPER PERENNIAL EDITION PUBLISHED 2011.
FIRST HARPER PERENNIAL OLIVE EDITION PUBLISHED 2016.

The Library of Congress has catalogued a previous edition of this book as follows:

Roosevelt, Eleanor, 1884–1962
   You learn by living.
   Reprint. Originally published: 1st ed. New York : Harper, 1960. With new introd.
   Includes index.
   1. Conduct of life.   2. Roosevelt, Eleanor, 1884–1962.   I. Title.
BJ1581.2.R64   1983   158'.1   83-6838
   ISBN 0-662-24494-7 (pbk.)

ISBN 978-0-06-256472-6 (Olive Edition)

16 17 18 19 20   RRD   10 9 8 7 6 5 4 3 2 1

*To my grandchildren and great-grandchildren
in the hope that sometime they may find
a little help in these pages*

I want to express my very warm gratitude
and thanks to Miss Elinore Denniston,
whose work with me made this book possible,
and also to Miss Nannine Joseph for her
wise counsel in any work that I undertake.

E. R.

Contents

Foreword

Over the years I have received hundreds of thousands of letters—at the present time about a hundred a day. The vast majority of them contain questions that run the gamut from the personal problems that beset us all to the world problems that, now and henceforth, also beset us all. What these letters add up to is this: What have you learned from life that might help solve this or that difficulty?

Of course, no one is equipped with such wisdom. No one is adequate to give such blanket answers. No one finds ultimate solutions. But the questions are questions we all meet in our lives; they are questions we must all answer in some way. Not with finality, for life is too fluid, too *alive* for that. So I have been forced to stop and think through some of the questions, to try to find my own answers, to discover what I have learned by living.

When one attempts to set down in bald words any answers one has found to life problems, there is a great risk of appearing to think that one's answer is either the only one or the best one. This, of course, would be nonsense. I have no such all-inclusive wisdom to offer, only a few guideposts that have proved helpful to me in the course of a long life. Perhaps they may steer someone away from the pitfalls into which I stumbled or help them to avoid the mistakes I have made. Or perhaps one can learn only by one's own mistakes. The essential thing is to learn.

Learning and living. But they are really the same thing, aren't they? There is no experience from which you can't learn something. When you stop learning you stop living in any vital and meaningful sense. And the purpose of life, after all, is to live it, to taste experience to the utmost, to reach out eagerly and without fear for newer and richer experience.

You can do that only if you have curiosity, an unquenchable spirit of adventure. The experience can have meaning only if you understand it. You can understand it only if you have arrived at some knowledge of yourself, a knowledge based on a deliberately and usually painfully acquired self-discipline, which teaches you to cast out fear and frees you for the fullest experience of the adventure of life.

My own life has been crowded with activity and, best of all, with people. I have seen them wrest victory from defeat; I have seen them conquer fear and come out strong and free; I have seen them turn empty lives into full and productive ones.

I honor the human race. When it faces life head-on, it can almost remake itself.

One's philosophy is not best expressed in words; it is expressed in the choices one makes. In stopping to think through the meaning of what I have learned, there is much

I believe intensely, much I am unsure of. But this, at least, I believe with all my heart: In the long run, we shape our lives and we shape ourselves. The process never ends until we die. And the choices we make are ultimately our own responsibility.

Hyde Park
January, 1960

chapter 1

Learning to Learn

One of the most intriguing questions that comes to me in the mail is: "How did you plan your career and how did you prepare for it?" I always feel perfectly inadequate to answer this because I never planned a career and never prepared for it. To this day I do not feel I have had a career. What I have done is to live every experience to the utmost.

As I look back, I think probably the factor which influenced me most in my early years was an avid desire, even before I was aware of what I was doing, to experience all I could as deeply as I could.

I must have been no more than five when I went on a trip to Italy with my father and mother. In Venice, my father invited me to ride in a gondola and he paid the gondolier to sing. Some sort of fiesta was going on at the time and people were tossing flowers. I can still remember that ride. Baby that I was, I had the sense to feel it as an experience.

Everything I did with my father remains in my memory today, a vivid moment not to be forgotten. I remember standing on the edge of Vesuvius with him while he threw in a penny, which came back covered with lava. There was excitement and wonder in that. He took me through the ruins and showed me a petrified loaf of bread and told me how a long-vanished civilization had lived. But it wasn't dead history. It became vivid to me. These were living people, and as I learned about them they seemed as real as the ones about me.

What I have learned from my own experience is that the most important ingredients in a child's education are curiosity, interest, imagination, and a sense of the adventure of life. You will find no courses in which these are taught; and yet they are the qualities that make all learning rewarding, that make all life zestful, that make us seek constantly for new experience and deeper understanding. They are also the qualities that enable us to continue to grow as human beings to the last day of our life, and to continue to learn.

By learning, of course, I mean a great deal more than so-called formal education. Nobody can learn all he needs to know. Education provides the necessary tools, equipment by which we learn how to learn. The object of all our education and all the development which is a part of education is to give every one of us an instrument which we can use to acquire information at any time we need it.

I remember certain milestones in learning how to learn.

As far as training my memory was concerned, that began very young. I loved poetry and I would often learn it while I was dressing and undressing. When I was quite young, I had a French teacher who made us learn by heart a good part of the New Testament in French. This was helpful later when I was in a French school in England. The French mistress had us listen to her read a French poem, of perhaps eight lines, and repeat it after the first reading. At first I could not do it, but gradually I was able to manage fairly well.

She taught us history and, though we were only fifteen or sixteen, I imagine her methods were more like those of a college professor. We sat on little chairs on either side of her fireplace, over which maps were hung. She would turn to the map of the area of the world we were learning about and tell us to remember our geography because it affected history. Then she would give us a list of books to read and take up the particular point we were studying, giving us as many different lights on the period as she thought we could understand. Our requirement was to do our reading and then write a paper on the assignment.

The English girls were apt to remember what she had said and repeat it in their papers. I can still see her, as one of the girls was reading her paper aloud, standing over her with a long ruler in her hand, taking away the paper, and tearing it up.

"You are giving me back what I gave you," she said, "and it does not interest me. You have not sifted it through your own intelligence. Why was your mind given you but to think things out for yourself?"

It became a challenge for me to think about all the different sides of a situation and try to find new points that Mlle. Souvestre had not covered, points that had not even been covered in our books. It was rather exciting to have these questions come to my mind as I read and I can remember now how pleased I was when she would ask me to leave my paper with her and later return it with the comment, "Well thought out, but have you forgotten this or that point?"

That was an imaginative method of education and most valuable.

We obtain our education at home, at school, and, most important, from life itself. The learning process must go on as long as we live. Nothing alive can stand still, it goes forward or back. Life is interesting only as long as it is a process of growth; or, to put it another way, we can grow only as long as we are interested.

For some years now there has been considerable conflict in educational circles about what and how children should be taught. The old system was to serve two purposes: to discipline the mind and to provide young people with a background of knowledge about the past, history, philosophy, and the arts.

More recently, the influence of Dewey has been powerful in effecting a change in orientation. It is not so important, according to this school, to provide the child with a background of general culture. The essential thing is to relate every fact learned to the tangible world around him. The purpose of his education is to explain to him the things he can feel and see and touch and experience in his daily life.

Carried to an extreme, the progressive method has not attempted to direct the child in any direction in which he does not want to go. Unless he enjoys it or sees a value in it, he is not forced to accept the discipline.

Both methods have their value. Of course, it is useful to relate the child to his immediate surroundings, to have him understand them and their functioning. It is never enough, it seems to me, to teach a child mere information. In the first place, we have to face the fact that no one can acquire all there is to learn about any subject. What is essential is to train the mind so that it is capable of finding facts as it needs them, train it to learn how to learn. If, later on, a child must acquire a foreign language he should have a background of training to enable him to sit down and concentrate on mastering the language. If he must do research, he should have discipline and training in how to do research. It is not enough to have done one or more pieces of research. He must have mastered the technique.

The essential thing is that he is so trained that he can use his mind as a tool, a supple instrument to dig out the facts as he needs them. But facts, after all, are a comparatively small part of education. They are a small part of the thing broadly known as culture.

Every now and then, I receive rather pathetic letters from young women who have married men who either have come from a different background or have climbed fast in their professional careers and belong to cultural worlds in which the young wives feel alien.

"How," they ask me, "can I educate myself so that I will

fit in with my husband's family and friends? What ought I to learn?"

I answer them as best I can, inadequately, I am afraid, because it is difficult to give anyone a list of books which, in themselves, will provide him or her with culture. I tell them that they should read at least a few of the classics, translations of the Greek philosophers, and some of the old Greek plays. They can read books on history, art, philosophy, biography; they should be familiar with some of the best fiction. All these, of course, will add to their background and give them at least a glimpse of the intellectual framework of our past.

But the answer must go farther than that. What counts, in the long run, is not what you read; it is what you sift through your own mind; it is the ideas and impressions that are aroused in you by your reading. It is the ideas stirred in your own mind, the ideas which are a reflection of your own thinking, which make you an interesting person.

Book education cannot accomplish this by itself. It needs the supplement and the stimulus of the exchange of ideas with other people. In particular, it means learning from other people. There is no human being from whom we cannot learn something if we are interested enough to dig deep.

As a young woman, I was very conscious that I did not have a formal education of the kind many children in the United States have. I did not realize that my mother had given me one thing that was going to be useful all the rest of my life. She had made me learn French before I learned English by the simple device of providing me with a French nurse. I learned both languages simultaneously and though I have at times gone for long periods without reading or speaking French, it takes only a short time to pick it up again when I am where I hear it spoken constantly.

That gave me a taste for languages and though, like many other children, I was bored by Latin, which was considered essential at the time, and I cannot say that Caesar's Gallic Wars were ever very interesting, I soon came to discover that in the thing which I greatly enjoyed, the acquiring of languages, Latin was of positive help.

I had studied in private classes until I was sent abroad for three years of English and French education. On the whole it was good education, in some ways almost on a college level. But it was different.

When I came home I was aware that there were great gaps in my knowledge. I married very young and came into a different atmosphere, and began to meet a great variety of people. Knowing my own deficiencies, I made a game of trying to make people talk about whatever they were interested in and learning as much as I could about their particular subject. After a while I had acquired a certain technique for picking their brains. It was not only great fun but I began to get an insight into many subjects I could not possibly have learned about in any other way. And, best of all, I discovered vast fields of knowledge and experience that I had hardly guessed existed.

This, I think, is one of the most effective and rewarding forms of education. The interest is there, lurking somewhere in another person. You have only to seek for it. It will make every encounter a challenge and it will keep alive one of the most valuable qualities a person has—curiosity.

Ruth Bryan Rohde once told me that she found it very useful, if she was sitting next to a person whose interests she knew nothing about, to begin going through the alphabet. A is for ants. "Mr. Jones, are you interested in the life of the ant?" He might not be interested in the ant but at least he was startled and amused.

At the time the idea entertained me, though I doubted that it would ever serve my purpose. But a time came when the alphabet saved me from sitting in utter silence throughout a whole meal.

My husband and I were landing at Boston with President and Mrs. Wilson, after the conference from which the President was bringing the first draft of the League of Nations treaty. Governor and Mrs. Calvin Coolidge met the President and his wife. Suddenly we were informed that President Wilson would have to speak that afternoon, so it was impossible for him to lunch with the Governor as the latter had planned. My husband and I were to go as substitutes.

I saw my husband was having a perfectly delightful time at the other end of the table with Mrs. Coolidge, who was talkative and gracious. I struggled with a partner who never did anything but grunt. I tried every letter of the alphabet but I did not succeed even in startling Governor Coolidge, let alone amusing him, no matter how outrageous a subject I suggested.

As I remember it, we finished our dessert in absolute silence, after I had exhausted the alphabet. I was most uncomfortable but he was quite happy. He preferred to eat in peace and quiet and he saw no reason for saying a word.

There is a wonderful word, *why?*, that children use. All children. When they stop using it, the reason, too often, is that no one bothered to answer them, no one tried to keep alive one of the most important attributes a person can have: interest in the world around him. No one fostered and cultivated the child's innate sense of the adventure of life.

One of the things I believe most intensely is that every child's *why* should be answered with care—and with respect. If you do not know the answer, and you often will not, then take the child with you to a source to find the answer. This may be a dictionary or encyclopedia which he is too young to use himself, but he will have had a sense of participation in finding the answer.

But if you brush aside the eager question, the only way the young child has of learning to understand his world, and say, "I don't know. . . . Don't bother me; can't you see I am busy?" or, worse still, "What a silly question!" something bad will happen in time. If the child's curiosity is not fed, if his questions are not answered, he will stop asking questions. And then, by the time he is in his middle twenties, he will stop wondering about all the mysteries of his world. His curiosity will be dead.

For curiosity, interest, and a longing to know more and more types of experience are the qualities that stimulate a desire to know about life and to understand it. They provide the zest that makes it possible to meet any situation as an adventure. Without that spirit of adventure, life can be a dull business. With it, there is no situation, however limiting, physically or economically, which cannot be filled to the brim with interest. Indeed, without interest, it is almost impossible to continue to learn; certainly, it is impossible to continue to grow.

Now and then, I am surprised to read of the death of someone I have known, because I thought he or she had died long ago. Actually, he had only stopped growing. Other people, against tremendous handicaps, continue to grow. I am thinking especially of one of my aunts, Mrs. Cowles. She became so helplessly crippled by arthritis that she could not move. Every day she was dressed and lifted into a chair where she remained until she was put to bed at night.

Then her hearing began to fail. In time, she was almost completely deaf. The mechanical hearing aids of today were unknown. She had a crude sort of box placed on a table before her into which one shouted in order to be heard.

She might have become an ingrown, self-pitying invalid; dependent for everything on the people around her, with her interests enclosed within the narrow circle of herself. But she didn't. There was not a young member of the family who would not have traveled any distance to be with her. Into that box on the table were shouted their confidences, their problems, their doubts and anxieties. And always they met with a response.

She did not burden them or herself with her own bitter handicaps. She turned all her attention outward upon her young visitors. She was genuinely interest desire to know about them, to understand th help them find a way of coping with their dilem broad understanding and a wisdom that was bot pathetic and kindly. And she had a rarer quality—she could listen.

We all know the frustrating experience of trying to talk out a problem and discovering that our chosen confidant is giving us only divided attention, or frankly thinking of something else, or waiting to get in a word about some problem of his or her own. But you could talk to my aunt, knowing she really listened, that she was trying to understand, that if you wanted advice she would call on all her wisdom to help you.

This is rare to find. So many older people, particularly in dealing with the young, feel that they know all the answers. They don't discuss things with you. They tell you. But my aunt kept, until her death, the elasticity of her mind, though she had so long lost the elasticity of her body.

Today, many old people who were young in those days and went to her for advice and understanding still wonder, in a dilemma, what she would have said, what she would have advised, and are aware of an ever-recurring sense of loss that she can no longer tell them.

What made my aunt the rare and useful person she was can be explained only, I think, by the fact that she never lost her curiosity, her interest was never dimmed, she still reached out for new experience and welcomed it. Without those qualities she could never have managed to continue to grow and to increase in depth of understanding. Nor could she have been, as she was, in spite of crippling handicaps, a happy woman.

Her younger sister, Mrs. Douglas Robinson, was a poet. Perhaps she has no claim to live among the immortals but she wrote some things that I still like to read, and, about those she loved, she wrote with astonishing insight. During the First World War she wrote a poem about Mrs. Cowles, called "Soldier of Pain,"* which epitomized my aunt.

Not in the trenches, torn by shot and shelling,
    Not on the plain,
Bombed by the foe; but calm and unrebelling,
    Soldier of Pain!

Facing each day, head high with gallant laughter,
    Anguish supreme;
What accolade in what divine hereafter
    Shall this redeem?

Through the long night of racked, recurrent waking,
    Till the long day,
Fraught with distress, brings but the same heartbreaking
    Front for the fray.

In a far land our Nation's patriots, willing,
    Fought, and now lie—
But you—as brave—a harder fate fulfilling,
    Dare *not* to die!

---

* From *The Poems of Corinne Roosevelt Robinson*, published by Charles Scribner's Sons.

One thing life has taught me: if you are interested, you never have to look for new interests. They come to you. They will gravitate as automatically as the needle to the north. Somehow, it is unnecessary, in any cold-blooded sense, to sit down and put your head in your hands and plan them. All you need to do is to be curious, receptive, eager for experience. And there's one strange thing: when you are genuinely interested in one thing, it will always lead to something else.

It is here, I think, that the most important phase of education appears, in the capacity to learn from each thing you see, from each fact you acquire, from each experience you have, from each person you meet. And nothing you learn, however wide of the mark it may appear at the time, however trivial, is ever wasted. In all my life, nothing I have ever learned has failed to be useful to me at some time or other, often in the most unexpected way and in some quite unforeseen context.

I am often asked how I acquired an interest in politics. My usual answer is that it is because of my uncle, Theodore Roosevelt, and my husband. But, actually, I think a little incident that occurred when my husband and I were on our first trip to Europe after our wedding stimulated my curiosity about government and politics.

We were staying with Ronald Ferguson and his wife, Lady Helen. She was the daughter of a statesman and the wife of a man who had been Privy Seal for Scotland and Governor-General of Australia. She had taken part in innumerable campaigns and she was keen about politics.

As I came into the living room for tea one afternoon while

we were there, she looked up and said, "There's one question
I have always wanted to ask some American. Will you please
explain the relationship between your states and your federal
government?"

I was floored. No one had taught me how my own government worked. I was saved because at that moment my
husband came in. I said, "Darling, Lady Helen would like to
know the relationship between the states and the federal government."

He gave her a full answer and I became aware of a real gap
in my education. I made up my mind to find out as soon as
possible how my own government functioned so I would not
be embarrassed in this way again.

Franklin knew my problem quite well and his eyes twin-
kled as he gave the answer. He had saved me, but so far as our
personal relationship was concerned, we righted the balance
a day or so later in the north of Scotland when we went to stay
in the Dower House up in the Highlands with old Mrs. Ferguson and her son Hector. They asked me to open the flower
show. I, who had never spoken five words in public, was hor-
rified. I could not do it. So my husband was asked to do it. He
agreed, though he was somewhat taken aback when he was
asked to say something about the way we cook vegetables in
the United States.

He answered promptly that we cook all vegetables in
cream—this to people in the Highlands of Scotland! I could
not stop him. He embellished his theme and pointed out
in elaborate detail the virtues of this kind of cooking. Afterward he was rather surprised at the feeble applause that

greeted his speech. I told him I thought we had come out about even.

This part of learning—learning as you go—gives life its salt. And this, too, comes back primarily to interest. *You must be interested in anything that comes your way.*

Right here, some of you will shrug and say, "It's different for you. You've had an interesting life. But in my town—or my family—or my limited circumstances—"

Then I remember my aunt limited to a chair in which she could not move, to the physical barrier of four unchanging walls, to the deafness that could so easily have shut her off from life. And yet life came to her, sought her out. Best of all, it needed her.

Never, perhaps, have any of us needed as much as we do today to use all the curiosity we have, needed to seek new knowledge, needed to realize that no knowledge is terminal. For almost everything in our world is new, startlingly new. None of us can afford to stop learning or to check our curiosity about new things, or to lose our humility in the face of new situations.

If we can keep that flexibility of mind, that hospitality toward new ideas, we will be able to welcome the new flow of thought from wherever it comes, not resisting it; weighing and evaluating and exploring the strange new concepts that confront us at every turn.

We cannot shut the windows and pull down the shades; we cannot say, "I have learned all I need to know; my opinions are fixed on everything. I refuse to change or to consider these new things." Not today. Not any more.

Each generation supposes that the world was simpler for the one before it. The Victorians—or a portion of them, for some of their scientists changed much of man's vision of his world and himself, however much he resisted the idea—often felt that they had arrived at terminal knowledge on government, history, economics, science, social values, and the class system. A nice, neat, unchanging world. But where is it now?

Today, living and learning must go hand in hand. Each new bit of knowledge, each new experience is an extra tool in meeting new problems and working them out. It takes everything we can acquire to help us understand the new situations, the new problems that are arising on all sides.

If this sounds heavy and oppressive, then the essential point has been missed. Learning can be a game. Imagination, for instance, is always a game. I think it would be interesting to analyze a little bit what imagination is. Actually, it is the power to use whatever you have become conscious of and to project yourself beyond what you know into new situations and new thoughts, and develop them, so that you can see things in your mind's eye which you have never actually seen.

Because they have so little, children must rely on imagination rather than experience. They naturally live in a dream world. I was not a happy child so I learned, earlier than most, how important the happy moments are. Like most unhappy children, I lived a dream life in which everything was ordered to my liking and in which, of course, I was the heroine. My father was always the hero. He was good looking and charming. In the eyes of the child I was he had no faults and no weaknesses. For many years, he embodied all the qualities I looked for in a man. The things I saw and did with him stand out vividly among the somewhat gray days of my childhood. I experienced them so intensely that all I learned from them became a part of my life.

For years and years, I lived in that dream world with my father. I was lonely and he was the person I loved best and I felt that he loved me. I carried on a day-by-day story, which was the realest thing in my life. How many afternoons I skated away from my governess along Fifth Avenue, so that I could tell my story to myself without the jar of outside interruptions.

I had had some experiences with which to feed my dreams. I had been abroad. I had lived in the country as well as the city. I had met a number of people, my parents' friends. But chiefly I had my father's letters—he was rarely in the same city with me—in which he told me of all the wonderful things we were going to do together.

I was nine when he died, but my dream story went on without a break. He had often told me that someday we would travel to distant parts of the world together, so I made up stories of traveling with him, nourishing them with details from all that I had read.

This power of imagination is a kind of defense in childhood. You get away from the realities. It makes you important to yourself. If used correctly, it makes it more possible for you later on to imagine what other people are like and what they think and feel. It helps to keep you curious, anxious to understand what is going on around you.

Of course, unless it is checked, imagination can remain

only a means of escape; but if it is nourished and directed, it can become a flame that lights the way to new things, new ideas, new experience.

I think a child is particularly fortunate if he grows up in a family where his imagination can be fed, where there are a variety of intellectual interests, where someone loves music, or does amateur painting, or is engrossed in literature, reading aloud perhaps, or just exchanging comments about what is being read.

I think it is a tremendous loss to a child to grow up in a family without conversation. Naturally, there are always trivial things, plans and details to be talked over. But there should be general discussion of ideas as well, of the fantastic things that are happening all over the world, of new discoveries in science and archaeology, of local or distant problems and their possible solution, of anything that keeps before the child the realization that life is an exciting business, that it is to be approached in a spirit of adventure.

I was always glad that my husband loved to have the boys argue with him. Often he demolished them in one statement, but the heated discussion was stimulating to them all. To this day the boys continue to argue with each other, finding a mutual stimulus in the exchange of ideas and opinions.

Good talk, indeed, is important not only as a part of family life but as a part of education. A child from that kind of family life can go out into school or his business or profession much better prepared both to contribute and to absorb new impressions.

This kind of education provides a constant sharpening of

the child's awareness of his world, a constant challenge to develop and express his opinions, a constant intensification of zest for experience.

Along with the stimulus of good talk, of the education that comes almost unconsciously from casual discussion of books read, from a gradual knowledge of music heard as part of daily life, there is also the great value of surrounding a child with objects of beauty, which, almost imperceptibly, help to form taste.

These don't have to be original paintings by the old masters or *objets d'art* of great rarity and value. There are copies that cost only a few pennies. I have often thought, as I walked up the Champs-Elysées toward the Place de la Concorde and watched the children playing, that the thing we call French culture may be due to the fact that French children can play, surrounded by the things of the past, palaces of bygone kings, statues, remembrances of history. These become part of the child's background, because he played ball surrounded by them. Later, he will know who Napoleon and Jeanne d'Arc were because he saw their statues every day as he walked to and from the park. He may be more interested in the Guignol, but when he grows up he will have absorbed, unconsciously, the impact and meaning of his surroundings. That is what makes a nation's culture.

The kinds of things with which you surround a child will sink into his consciousness. Years ago, when I made Val-Kill furniture, copies of American antiques, I gave some pieces to my children for their own rooms at home so that, when they married, they would have some furniture of their own. I discovered an interesting thing. The children who had these replicas of antiques began, without being taught, to recognize finish, the beauty of wood, how the pieces were put together. If a drawer was fitted and pegged instead of being nailed together they noticed it right away. They became very discriminating.

However, while it is important to surround a child with objects that have beauty, it is also important to be sure that he understands them. It is quite possible that he may be confused without your ever guessing it.

Not long ago, I was going through the nursery at the big house at Hyde Park with my grandson Curtis. On the wall there was a published print of Theodore Roosevelt.

That portrait of Uncle Ted, he confessed, had confused and baffled him for years. He knew that his grandfather was President of the United States, but people would look at Uncle Ted's portrait and say that *he* was President. The child was bewildered and tried in vain to sort it out in his own mind. But he had never revealed his puzzlement to anyone else.

Perhaps the most essential thing for a continuing education is to develop the capacity *to know what you see and to understand what it means*. Many people seem to go through life without seeing. They do not know how to look around them. Only when you have learned that can you really continue to learn about people, about conditions, about your own locality.

As an example, many years ago the Consumers League asked me to check on conditions in department stores. I made my report. It was valueless.

"But," I was asked, "do these women have any stools to sit on behind the counter when they are not waiting on customers or must they stand all day?"

For years I had gone to department stores, I had seen women behind counters. It had never occurred to me that perhaps they could never sit down and rest. I hadn't looked. And if I had looked, I would not have understood what it meant until someone else pointed out its meaning.

When I began—so slowly—actually to look around me and to try to understand the meaning of what I saw, everything I encountered became more interesting and more valuable. It was like a two-dimensional picture seen in three dimensions, with depth.

If you can develop this ability to see what you look at, to understand its meaning, to readjust your knowledge to this new information, you can continue to learn and to grow as long as you live and you'll have a wonderful time doing it.

chapter 2

Fear—the Great Enemy

Fear has always seemed to me to be the worst stumbling block which anyone has to face. It is the great crippler. Looking back, it strikes me that my childhood and my early youth were one long battle against fear.

I was an exceptionally timid child, afraid of the dark, afraid of mice, afraid of practically everything. Painfully, step by step, I learned to stare down each of my fears, conquer it, attain the hard-earned courage to go on to the next. Only then was I really free.

Of all the knowledge that we acquire in life this is the most difficult. But it is also the most rewarding. With each victory, no matter how great the cost or how agonizing at the time, there comes increased confidence and strength to help meet the next fear.

I do not know any way of doing this except through self-discipline. In educational circles there is always a great deal of talk about how much discipline should be imposed. I do not know the answer, but I do know that the discipline one imposes on oneself is the only sure bulwark one has against fear. It is a lesson I had to learn at a painfully early age.

My grandmother brought me up from the time I was seven. Because she had been overindulgent with her own children, she decided that my younger brother and I must be taught to obey. She proceeded on the theory that it is wiser to say "no" than "yes" to children.

She believed that a daily cold sponge bath kept one from catching cold and I took cold sponge baths for years. She believed that if I caught cold or had a headache it was a result of my own foolishness and that I should be expected to keep myself in good health. All this was spartan treatment and it was, I think, carried to excess, but I must confess that even today I feel that I am responsible for using common sense in keeping myself in good health.

All this was imposed discipline. I learned in time that when I wanted very much to do things I was more than apt to be told "no." So I learned self-discipine as a kind of defense. I learned to protect myself from disappointment by not asking for what I wanted.

There were things I wanted so much, things like love and affection. I was conscious, as only a very young girl can be, of the fact that I did not have the looks of my aunts or my beautiful mother. I was the ugly duckling. I had such an intense longing for approval and love that it forced me to acquire self-descipline. Undoubtedly, this stood me in good stead in later life but I had to attain it much earlier than most people do.

I had to make a difficult choice: I was afraid of everything, but, on the other hand, I wanted to do things that would win me the affection I craved. So I had to stare down my fears.

I can remember vividly an occasion when I was living in my grandmother's house on Thirty-seventh Street in New York City. One of my aunts was ill and asked for some ice, which was kept in the icebox out of doors in the back yard.

I was so frightened that I shook. But I could not refuse to go. If I did that, she would never again ask me to help her and I could not bear not to be asked.

I had to go down alone from the third floor in the dark, creeping through the big house, which was so hostile and unfamiliar at night, in which unknown terrors seemed to lurk. Down to the basement, shutting a door behind me that cut me off from the house and safety. Out in the blackness of the back yard.

I suffered agonies of fear that night. But I learned that I could face the dark and it never again held such horror for me.

I think my grandmother quite unwittingly let fears take root in me because she left so many questions unanswered. She never told me anything, but she allowed me to read anything I wanted in the library, which held a great many books. A number of them were on theological subjects, which did not attract me, though I still remember the terror aroused by the Gustave Doré illustrations of the Bible.

Reading all the way through Dickens and Scott, I came upon much material which I could not understand. Although I lived in the family with young uncles and aunts, they did not consider it their business to tell me much about life. As a result, I would face members of my family at awkward moments with questions which they did not want to answer. The book I was reading would promptly disappear. No matter how much I looked or asked, no one had seen it. I never realized that it had been removed, so I went on searching. As I grew in knowledge, I would find the book again and understand what I had been reading and why my questions had not been answered.

I can remember one day coming home from the class which was my source of information on many subjects, chiefly from other children, all of whom were well-brought-up little girls. I said to my grandmother, "What is the meaning of whore? It is in the Bible."

"It is not a word that little girls should use," she told me severely.

Later on, my school friends enlightened me.

The fact of being free to read while not being able to understand what I was reading only whetted my curiosity. While I cannot say my grandmother enlightened me, her negative method made me seek enlightenment on many subjects she was far from wanting me to know about.

I remember once being sent to a church fair and being given money to spend. Instead, I spent my money for a ticket to *Tess of the d'Urbervilles*, which my young aunts had seen. I had been told that I was too young to go.

But the withholding of information from a child either frustrates him or makes him seek it for himself. And the trouble with the latter method is that it is apt to make the child feel both guilty and dishonest.

I found myself enmeshed in a series of lies, trying to explain why I brought nothing home from the fair. At length, it was easier to own up and take my punishment. Stealing and lying, they told me, were unforgivable sins. For three days, no one spoke to me. To a child who wanted above everything else to be loved, this was a terrible punishment.

None the less, I went on lying, more or less, out of fear, until I went to boarding school abroad at fifteen. I can remember now the wonder and the freedom I experienced when I realized that I could start with a clean slate, that there was nothing to be afraid of.

Through most of my early life that childish fear persisted, the terror of displeasing the people I lived with. I look back now with amazement on the dreadful day after I was married. Franklin had given me one of his precious first editions to look at. In some inconceivable way, I tore one page a little. I held it in my hands, while cold shivers went up and down my spine. Finally, I made myself tell him what I had done. He looked at me with bewilderment and some amusement. "If you had not done it, I probably would. A book is made to be read, not to be held." What I had dreaded I don't know, but I remember my vast relief. That was the beginning of my becoming more mature about my fears of displeasing people.

The encouraging thing is that every time you meet a situation, though you may think at the time it is an impossibility and you go through the tortures of the damned, once you have met it and lived through it you find that forever after you are freer than you ever were before. If you can live through that you can live through anything. You gain strength, courage, and confidence by every experience in which you really stop to look fear in the face.

You are able to say to yourself, "I lived through this horror. I can take the next thing that comes along."

The danger lies in refusing to face the fear, in not daring to come to grips with it. If you fail anywhere along the line it will take away your confidence. You must make yourself succeed every time. *You must do the thing you think you cannot do.*

Like too many people of my generation I grew up with a fear of insanity and no real understanding of it. During the First World War, I was living in Washington, where my husband was Assistant Secretary of the Navy. The Red Cross asked me to visit St. Elizabeth's Hospital, where the Navy had a big installation for boys who had gone temporarily or permanently insane.

I cannot do this, I thought. I was terrified of insanity. Then I realized that I was the Assistant Secretary's wife. This was my job. I had to do it whether I could do it or not.

The first time I went to the ward with the doctor, he unlocked a door, we went in, and then he locked it behind us. Locked in with the insane! I wanted to bang at the door, to get out. But I was ashamed of myself. I would not have shown my terror for the world.

It was a long ward with men, some of them in cubicles chained to their beds, and a strange sound permeating the whole place. The men were talking and mumbling to themselves, not conversation, just private thoughts revealed in an endless series of monologues.

At the end of the ward, standing where the sun coming through the window touched his golden hair, stood a handsome young man. He did not see us. He saw nothing but some private vision of his own. He kept muttering.

"What is he saying?" I asked the doctor.

"He keeps repeating the orders at Dunkirk to go to the shelters."

"Will he get over it?"

"I don't know," the doctor said flatly.

I watched the boy struggling with his private hell and my imaginary fear seemed shameful. It was one more hurdle to climb over but it had to be done. That, at least, I need never fear again.

One thing I learned by those visits to the Naval Hospital helped me enormously later on. Over and over, I met women there, young and old, who were obliged to confront situations they had never conceived of. They had to face the fact that their husbands or sons were temporarily or permanently affected mentally by the war. They met the problem in different ways, of course, most of them courageously, some of them magnificently. Often I became involved in the fate of a particular boy and some of them I followed for years after they left the hospital. To see how people could face what seemed to be an insurmountable disaster was a tremendous lesson.

*   *   *

Imaginary fears. Most of us, I suppose, are ridden by at least some imaginary fears. But I think it is as important to deal with these as it is with the fears based on a reasonable foundation. They often do us more harm.

Timidity and shyness are fears of this sort. Unimportant, perhaps, but they are crippling to self-confidence and to achievement.

> Our doubts are traitors
> And make us lose the good we oft might win
> By fearing to attempt.

Looking back, I see how abnormally timid and shy I was as a girl. As long as I let timidity and shyness dominate me I was half paralyzed. But again self-discipline was the great help. I had to learn to face people and I could not do it so long as I was obsessed with fears about myself, which is the usual situation with shyness. I learned a liberating thing. If you will forget about yourself, whether or not you are making a good impression on people, what they think of you, and you will think about them instead, you won't be shy.

Do the things that interest you and do them with all your heart. Don't be concerned about whether people are watching you or criticizing you. The chances are that they aren't paying any attention to you. It's your attention to yourself that is so stultifying. But you have to disregard yourself as completely as possible. If you fail the first time then you'll just have to try harder the second time. After all, there's no real reason why you should fail. Just stop thinking about yourself.

A spirit of adventure and the desire for experience did more than anything to help me master my shyness. I was terribly sensitive to what people would think and feel. But my desire to taste all of life and try to understand it was so intense that I went ahead, regardless of whether or not people were watching me or approving, and so slowly acquired a new sense of freedom and confidence.

Discipline of mind and body is one of the most difficult things one has to acquire, but in the long run it is a valuable ingredient of education and a tremendous bulwark in time of trouble. Certainly, it is essential in meeting defeats and re- covering from disaster. No matter how hard hit you are, you can face what has to be faced if you have learned to master your own fears.

Often people have asked me, "How do you recover from disaster?" I don't know any answer except the obvious one: You do it by meeting it and going on. From each you learn something, from each you acquire additional strength and confidence in yourself to meet the next one when it comes.

When things that happen to you are inevitable there is a kind of courage that comes from sheer desperation. If it is inevitable and has to be met, you can meet it. I remember when a friend of mine was expecting her first baby and I was expecting mine. One day she said, "I am really not afraid of having a baby. Everyone has to be born. If so many people can go through it successfully, why shouldn't I?"

I had not been expressing my own fear in words, as this would have shocked my husband and my mother-in-law. But in anticipating any new adventure, particularly when you have been told that it entails a great deal of pain, you are bound to wonder whether you will cope with it, how you will deal with the situation. My mother-in-law had told me about the Chinese women who sat on hard benches and never said a word through their entire ordeal, but this was not as encouraging as perhaps it should have been. I did realize, however, that I was expected to be completely cheerful, completely self-controlled, not in the least worried about having a baby. It was a perfectly normal procedure.

I never said anything, though I was afraid I might not conduct myself with proper self-control. But as that could not be decided until the event occurred and this was something I could do nothing about—the child would come when it would come, as inevitably as death itself, and there was no use trying to escape it—I found myself gradually acquiring the discipline I needed for the final ordeal. I never again was afraid of bearing a child.

A great deal of fear is a result of just "not knowing." We do not know what is involved in a new situation. We do not know whether we can deal with it. The sooner we learn what it entails, the sooner we can dissolve our fear.

It seems to me that I knew almost nothing when I was married. I was unequipped to handle any kind of situation. I had acquired social training and a respect for social duties because that had been drilled into me from childhood. But the daily problems of running a household were entirely beyond me.

I did not know how to cook. My grandmother had taught me how to run a household in her way, measuring out the flour and sugar and other supplies and turning them over to the servants who were to use them. But she did not—she could not—envisage a world without cooks. So the first time I faced a dinner party with the knowledge that the cook had just left without notice was a catastrophe I can still remember because it seemed to me the end of the world had come. I didn't know how to cope with the situation.

The first time a nurse left and a baby cried all evening I was frantic. Here was a disaster of major proportions and I didn't know what to do. (The doctor answered my wild appeals over the telephone with the dry comment, "Probably gas.")

I discovered, as everyone has to discover, sooner or later, that either I must learn how to deal with situations or I must go down in defeat, terrified at the possibility that something would happen.

Fortunately, I had with me at the birth of each child the same trained nurse, and she came back to me whenever she could when one of the children was ill. I acquired from her the principles of good health care and sound nursing technique, so that I was no longer terrified when anything unexpected happened and the children were ill with the various diseases of childhood. I knew I could handle it competently.

When the flu epidemic reached Washington in 1918, it proved to be a major catastrophe in the overcrowded city. Temporary shelters were put up for the thousands of victims, often in places without even cooking facilities. The Cabinet wives and the wives of the under secretaries agreed to supply food to certain of these shelters every day. My particular assignment was to provide large cans of soup for one particular shelter. I went there every day and came to know some of the people and to realize when there were curtains around a bed that someone was dying or had died.

I recognized how lonely these young patients must be, far away from family and homes. And I forgot to be afraid myself in my thankfulness that I could in some small way help them, and that my own family could be cared for safely in my own home.

Every member of my family came down with flu, my husband and all five children. I was able to get a nurse for Elliott, who also had pneumonia. The other five I nursed myself.

This was one of the occasions when I was grateful for my grandmother's stern training. I had kept myself in good condition and I was able to cope with nursing five members of my own family and to make my rounds with the soup, talking to the sick girls in the shelter. With a house filled with flu patients, I had no reason to fear infection from the outside.

Meeting smaller emergencies and learning to deal with them had given me the confidence to deal with this larger emergency. So, little by little, I found out how to do things. After each catastrophe you don't worry so much the next time, and each time you emerge stronger from your victory.

Later, when my husband was taken ill at Campobello, there was no nurse to be had because of a widespread epidemic of influenza. For two weeks, during the whole serious part of the illness, there was no one but me to look after him. I could never have met this disaster if it had not been for the experiences that had preceded it.

At the end of these two weeks, when it became evident

that my husband's condition was the result of something more serious than a chill, a polio specialist, Dr. Lovett, was brought by my husband's uncle, Fred Delano, from Newport, where he had been vacationing. He did not know there had been no one but me to handle the situation. When he discovered we had no nurse he arranged to have one sent from New York; after that, she was with our family for a long time.

After his careful examination, the doctor said, "This case has been given very good nursing." All the minor skirmishes against fear had resulted, after all, in a kind of victory.

There is another kind of fear that is prevalent. Very often people seem afraid to put their own capabilities to use, as though one could save one's abilities and draw interest on them. The only interest, of course, comes from spending. Or they believe that if they make use of their own assets, some demands will be made upon them.

"If I cannot do it," they think, "no one will expect me to try."

This particular kind of fear is impoverishing because such a person never dares to find out how much he is really capable of doing. I have heard so many young women say, "Oh, I could never make a speech. You mustn't ask that of me."

I remember my own feeling that this was a thing I could not possibly do. But Louis Howe felt that if I were to be active in politics it would be a way of keeping my husband's interest alive while he was recuperating from his illness.

"You can do anything you have to do," Louis Howe said firmly. "Get out and try."

I was a most unwilling victim. When I got up to speak I

was shaking with fear because I had no idea how to prepare a speech, how to talk, how to handle an audience.

Louis Howe sat in the back of the hall and watched me. When it was over he criticized everything I had done, particularly the fact that I had giggled every now and then, though there was nothing funny.

"Of course I did," I admitted. "I didn't know what to say next."

Little by little, he taught me how to organize a speech. A novice, he said, should write out the beginning and the end ("They have no terminal facilities") and put down the main body of the speech in notes.

"Never write it down," he warned me. "You will lose your audience." He added, "When you have said what you have to say—sit down."

For a long time, those were the only rules I had. I followed them meticulously. I, who thought I could not speak to anyone, learned that if you have something to say you can say it.

It is easy to declare, "I never could do this or that." You will find that it can be done. In doing it you not only free yourself from another shackling fear but you stretch your mental muscles and gain the freedom that comes with achievement.

Every time you meet a crisis and live through it, you make it simpler for the next time. If you draw back and say, "I am afraid to do that," because you might do or say something wrong or you might make a mistake, you will become timid and negative as a person.

Gradually, as I was more or less propelled into public life, I learned to develop ideas of my own and to act on them.

Obviously, it requires effort to use all your potentialities to the best of your ability, to stretch your horizon, to grasp every opportunity as it comes, but it is certainly more interesting than holding off timidly, afraid to take a chance, afraid to fail.

One of the problems all parents face is that of bringing up their children to be as free of fear as possible. Certainly you can't accomplish this unless you have developed a philosophy for yourself that is freed from fear. If you can give them a trust in God, they will have one sure way of meeting all the uncertainties of existence.

Next in importance is to determine when they are ready to take on the task of disciplining themselves without direct parental control. This is an important part of their education. We may find that they are not prepared to relinquish imposed discipline as soon as they think they are. But it seems to me that when they believe the time has come, they should be given an opportunity to find out whether they have acquired enough self-discipline to get along without the discipline which parents, teachers, and friends have been giving them.

I remember my mother-in-law telling me a story about my husband when he was ten years old. He came to his parents one day and said with a great sigh, "Oh, for freedom!"

"What do you mean?"

"For just one day I would like to be able to decide everything for myself."

They promptly told him if this was what he wished, he could have his day of freedom.

The next morning he started out without any directions and a whole day of freedom lay before him. By noon he returned and asked some questions.

"Why, Franklin, that is for you to decide. You wanted a day of freedom."

After a pause he said, "I am tired of freedom."

Often parents are loath to let their children discipline themselves and it requires discipline on their own part to do it. And I have observed, too, that much imposed discipline is an expression of our own fears. When my husband was in his forties, his mother still said, "Have you got your rubbers on?" As a result, he refused to wear them.

Believers in progressive education feel that children can be led to the right thing by persuasion and reason, even at a very early age. In some cases, the child is not yet prepared to reason at an early age and the method is not successful. On the other hand, I remember one particular case in which I felt that, without question, if you had the patience and persuasiveness and did not mind making life difficult for everyone else around, this can be a wonderful way to bring up a child. The results in this case have been very good. The child is today a successful example of what can be done by intelligence and patience. He is highly intelligent and close intellectually to an intelligent mother and father. In his early teens, he is accepting responsibility for himself.

No method is applicable to everyone. Human beings, fortunately, differ greatly among themselves. Many children actually are happier when decisions are made for them, when they are required to do certain things. In a large family it is essential to have certain laws that apply to all in order to prevent jealousy among children. They must feel that the discipline is the same for each, that the family rules are without exceptions. Otherwise, there is a sense of inequality and a feeling of unhappiness.

With most families and most children you must have a certain number of rules to live by, and a discipline that is accepted, if the child is to realize that he has certain obligations. This is an important part of self-discipline and an essential element of being a good citizen in a democracy. Actually, when you come to understand self-discipline you begin to understand the limits of freedom. You grasp the fact that freedom is never absolute, that it must always be contained within the framework of other people's freedom.

There is another fear problem which is growing more widespread and which, I think, we must do all we can to check at the source. Increasingly people are growing afraid of what is in store for the world. They wonder whether they should plan to go in for professions and build homes and bring up families.

"There is so little security," they say. "We don't know what to plan for."

Well, what security did our first settlers have when they embarked on the *Mayflower*? Only what they could create for themselves with their own courage, their own activities, their own trust in themselves to be able to meet any situations— all unknown, all threatening—that they might encounter. It is the only way anyone can plan his life.

Today the world faces a great challenge: on one side a government preserved by fear, on the other a government of free men. I haven't ever believed that anything supported by fear can stand against freedom from fear. Surely we cannot be so stupid as to let ourselves become shackled by senseless fears. The result of that would be to have a system of fear imposed on us.

Courage is more exhilarating than fear and in the long run it is easier. We do not have to become heroes overnight. Just a step at a time, meeting each thing that comes up, seeing it is not as dreadful as it appeared, discovering we have the strength to stare it down.

chapter 3

The Uses of Time

On one of the walls in the big house at Hyde Park hang the portraits of Franklin Delano and his wife Laura Astor Delano. They lived at Barrytown, New York, in a large house which they had built like an Italian villa. They had no children so his brother's children came to visit Aunt Laura. The story my mother-in-law always told about her when she wanted to give my children a lesson was that one day her young visitors came racing into the house, later than they were supposed to be.

"We didn't have time . . ." one of them began.

"You had all the time there was," the dour lady of the portrait answered them.

We have all the time there is. The problem is: How shall we make the best use of it? There are three ways in which I have been able to solve that problem: first, by achieving an inner calm so that I can work undisturbed by what goes on around me; second, by concentrating on the thing in hand; third, by arranging a routine pattern for my days that allots certain activities to certain hours, planning in advance for everything that must be done, but at the same time remaining flexible enough to allow for the unexpected. There is a fourth point which, perhaps, plays a considerable part in the use of my time. I try to maintain a general pattern of good health so that I have the best use of my energy whenever I need it.

For me, this solution has worked well and has enabled me for many years to carry on a vast number of activities, to maintain a household, and to do a great deal of traveling. Of course, no two people have the same demands on their time; no two patterns can be exactly alike. But, in general, I have found this system is flexible enough to be adapted to almost any purpose.

First of my own personal requirements is inner calm. This, I think, is an essential. One of the secrets of using your time well is to gain a certain ability to maintain peace within yourself so that much can go on around you and you can stay calm inside. In the last few years, I have been hearing increasingly about tension. Everyone seems to suffer from it. I do not recall ever hearing the word when I was a child. Perhaps this was because there were more big families and people had to learn to adjust to each other, to be calm in the face of all that was going on around them.

With a family of five children I had to learn to stay outwardly and inwardly calm. Even when they were quite young I seemed to have a number of interests and activities. Because my husband and my children naturally were of first importance, the other activities often had to be carried on in a room where any number of things were happening, with children playing on the floor, shouting, and making all kinds of noise. Either I could learn to continue with the reading, writing, or whatever I had to do in the midst of this turmoil, or I would have to relinquish it. In time, I learned to go ahead even when the room was filled with children.

I learned that the ability to attain this inner calm, regardless of outside turmoil, is a kind of strength. It saves an immense amount of wear and tear on the nervous system. In this oasis of peace you are better able to cope with the noisy and conflicting demands of young children without irritation or impatience.

Of course, sometimes you find yourself concentrating so completely that you are practically oblivious to what is going on around you. That is annoying to children and sometimes frustrating. I can remember having my skirt pulled and my arm joggled by children who wanted to ask a question or get permission to do something and were furious because Mother had not even heard their first request.

When my son James was seven or eight years old he was ill and afterward he remained rather nervous for some time. The doctor said he was to lie perfectly relaxed and quiet for an hour every day. I had him do it and planned to read aloud for a quiet hour. But I did not have him go off by himself to rest. It seemed important to me that he should learn to do this while he was among other people.

We made a rule that he was to lie perfectly flat on the floor with a pillow under his head and his arms extended, hanging loose. He was not to open his eyes during that hour, no matter what happened. This was tremendous discipline for a young child who instinctively wants to look up at every sound. But in time he was able to do it, to lie with closed eyes, undisturbed by any sound. In those few weeks he learned a great deal of self-control and detachment.

I know many people who find it impossible to do anything unless they have complete calm around them. This must be because they have never learned to gain an inner calm, an oasis of peace within themselves. It is possible, as I have discovered, to be relaxed and restful in spite of any amount of physical turmoil without. For a person who has a busy schedule which makes great demands on his time, this is an invaluable thing to acquire, because you will be able to use your time in the best possible way without being disturbed by every little thing, by having your nerves jangled or losing your trend of thought, or, most disrupting, fighting against and resenting the noise and the interruptions.

The second most important thing is to learn to concentrate, to give all your attention to the thing at hand, and then to be able to put it aside and go on to the next thing without confusion.

My husband said that being President of the United States meant that you saw more kinds of people, took up more subjects, and learned more about a variety of things than anyone else. But it required complete concentration on the person you were with and on what he was saying. When that person left the room, you pulled down a shade in your mind, and you were ready, with your attention free, for what the next person had to say. You might have to shift from banking to forestry but each subject had the attention and concentration it required and each, in turn, was put into the back of the mind, ready to be called upon when needed.

Actually, you can finish any task much quicker if you concentrate on it for fifteen minutes than if you give it divided attention for thirty. And, aside from the question of efficiency, it is distracting for anyone to have the impression that you are thinking of the person you just saw or the one you are to see next. The resulting interview is apt to serve little purpose.

I must admit, however, that even with the most careful planning for the best use of my time, I find myself frequently making mistakes and giving interviews to people whom I should have had sense enough beforehand not to see. Then I try to end the interview as quickly as possible.

For instance, a few months ago I saw a young woman who had a most laudable object. She wanted to raise money for crippled children and thought she had found a way to do it, but, unfortunately, this required my co-operation. She wrote, asking for an interview. I agreed to see her for half an hour on a hot summer afternoon in New York, and she came all the way from the state of Washington.

When she finally got down to explaining how her purpose was to be accomplished, she brought out an attractive little gold band with two black enamel or onyx lines on either side. She told me that many women who had been married and were widowed or divorced, particularly those who were still fairly young, found it difficult to wear their old wedding or engagement rings. This would mark them as being out of the market, so to speak. But if they could wear something distinctive to show they were open to approach, it would make life easier for them. How would I feel about wearing one of these rings?

I told her it might be useful to some people but I would not take any interest in it. She was deeply disappointed. Without my support, she could not carry out her plan. No manufacturer would take it unless I sponsored it. I suggested that she get the support of some organization, but I had to stick to my first decision. I succeeded in reaching my door at least ten minutes before my next appointment.

The next visitor could have been a nice retired farmer, but, as far as I could discover, he had spent his time living and working in YMCA's all over the world. When he got tired of the United States he went elsewhere, but something always drew him back. He had asked to see me because he was going to Oslo and needed some information only I could give him.

I was rather amused when he told me that many Scandinavians wanted to come and live in the United States and he did not know how to help them accomplish this. Could I find a way so that it could be arranged more easily?

I suggested mildly that only the immigration service and the people who made the laws on immigration could help him. I was helpless in this predicament.

In the course of conversation he told me of his work in various Y's, of how good people had been to him when he was ill, but that he always found in the long run that he had to come home, even though he had no family here. I discovered that actually I was taking the place of a family, someone to see before he started on his next adventure. He was getting to be an old man and it was lonely to live without having someone to whom he could talk about his life and his hope. He had thought up his question for me really out of his need to establish a relationship with someone, a need we find not only in the small child without a family but in an old man ending his active career.

A means of merchandising a product. A way of establishing an illusory link of human relationship. In both these cases I had wasted my time. Even with planning, no one ever has much defense against the time wasters.

Of course, any person who is going to accomplish a great deal finds it essential to organize his time. You cannot use your time to the best advantage if you do not make some sort of plan. I find that life is much more satisfactory when it forms a kind of pattern, though I do not believe in too rigid a pattern. In the first place, you will create a pretty uninteresting and sterile atmosphere if everything is set so rigidly that it cannot be changed. Inflexibility will make your life an unnecessary burden and it will also make it dull. Worst of all, it will make you a burden to other people.

I do feel, though, that you should know in general what you plan to do with your time, what you want to accomplish with it; begin your day at approximately the same hour and, if you have servants or employees, get them started with a definite knowledge of what they are expected to do. This prevents confusion and anxiety on the part of people who are not sure of what their duties are to be.

Very early in my marriage, I had to learn to organize my time. Because my husband and children came first, I arranged my schedule around them and their needs and various routines so that I could be at home when they were. And because I always had outside interests, I had to plan for the best use of my time. This proved to be excellent training for my later years when the pressures on my time were so greatly increased.

Perhaps I can make clear what I mean by having a pattern, but not too inflexible a pattern, by giving an example of how I organize my life differently in different places while maintaining still, roughly at least, a certain schedule and routine.

In the summer I have a big household and many guests staying with me, mostly children. Usually we breakfast at eight-thirty. Then my housekeeper and I go over meals and I arrange for her to shop if I am not going to do it. Generally I have some chores of my own to do as part of the regular work.

I look over the mail, sign what is ready, and write my column. When that is done I am free to plan whatever my guests want to do or, if I have other work on hand, I keep at that until lunchtime. Usually my guests want to go swimming or to visit the library and I often join in that.

After lunch in the country I try to arrange some time in which to finish my mail and to read. Sometimes, because of the pressure of engagements or plans for my guests, my mail must be finished at night after my guests have gone to bed. In the afternoons there is generally an engagement of some sort.

After dinner I am usually free to read or, if I have guests, talk. Then I finish my work later. Unless I get to bed too late I like to read in bed for a while.

In the city, my schedule is very different. I plan to do my column immediately after breakfast, look at my mail, and then get to my office at the American Association for the United Nations at ten, where I work as long as there is work to do.

This is the one organization devoted entirely to trying to inform the people of the United States about the United Nations, what it is and what it does. When I left as a government representative to the United Nations, I went to ask the executive director of the American Association whether I could be a volunteer on the staff and this position I have continued to hold.

Nearly always I have guests for lunch or go to lunch, as I have a number of board meetings that fall at the lunch hour.

When I can get home to sign the mail in the afternoon I do so. If this is impossible, I do it at night. Usually I have people in for tea and I try to rest before dinner.

As a rule, I go to some public function or see friends in the evenings. If I have no engagement I go to the theater, of which I am very fond, or hear music. Then I finish my mail because it must be on my secretary's desk in the morning.

This is the general pattern. Of course, it is frequently broken as it must be to allow for the unexpected things that come up, doing recordings, radio, television, and so forth.

But on the whole the basic routine remains the same, with certain hours laid out for work. The drawback of my kind of schedule is that it allows too little time for reading in New York, which I have to make up for as best I can at Hyde Park. I seem always to be behind with the pamphlets and reports that people send me to read, and even more behind with the reading I want to do for sheer pleasure.

When I go on trips the whole routine is broken, though the broad pattern remains the same. No matter where I go I am followed by the mail. On my return I am swamped for some days and have to spend far more hours at my desk.

I go on two kinds of trips. My job is to lecture or to travel for the AAUN. The organization trips take more time, for there are appointments, morning, afternoon, and evening. On a lecture tour, the chances are that some part of the day, at least, will be free, particularly in a strange city where there are no distractions, and I can use the time to catch up on reading. I always take something to read on plane trips.

My fourth rule for the best use of my time is to use common sense in health so that I can rely on my energy to carry me through even the most strenuous day. In a way, I have been singularly fortunate in my heritage. From the Roosevelts, the Halls, and the Livingstons I have inherited great vitality and a large capacity for both work and play. And I learned, as a small child, to follow a common-sense regime in living and to feel responsible for keeping myself in good health.

It is true that there are people who "enjoy" poor health, but they are exceptions. And yet many people seem to neglect the simple rules of hygiene, of adequate diet, and of periodical check-ups, that would enable them to get so much more out of living because of the upsurge of energy which they would feel.

All this requires a certain amount of self-discipline, but I have discovered that, important as self-discipline is to a child, it is increasingly important as one grows older. Then it is really essential for your well-being to regulate your life and your habits in a sensible way.

Of course, as the years go on I find that I grow more weary after a day filled to the hilt with activity, as most of mine are, plus a long evening of social activity followed by work. I have only two remedies for weariness: one is change and the other is relaxation. Change comes with the shift from my winter to my summer activities, with the influx of grand-children, grandnephews, and grandnieces. Being surrounded by active youngsters ranging in age from two or three to the late teens is strenuous, but it is always interesting and invig-orating. Age needs the company of youth, I think, and it al-ways does me good.

Change comes, too, in travel, in plane trips to many different and sometimes remote and intriguing parts of the world. As for relaxation, I have learned to get that as I go along, to sleep in a plane or even to catch a five-minute cat nap in my chair while waiting for someone. If the capacity for relaxation is there, if you can attain the ability to create your own inner calm, you can get your relaxation as you go along, no matter how active you may be.

Of course, all this presupposes that you not only want to know how to use your time but that you have some use for it.

I think almost anyone would agree that unless time is good for something it is good for nothing.

The most unhappy people in the world are those who face the days without knowing what to do with their time. But if you have more projects than you have time for, you are not going to be an unhappy person. This is as much a question of having imagination and curiosity as it is of actually making plans. Things will come to you if you have the interest in the first place.

I am constantly surprised to hear women say, "Now that my children have grown up and left home I don't know what to do with myself. Life seems so empty." How, they wonder, are they to find new interests, find something to fill the empty hours.

It seems to me that the real problem does not lie in diminished interests after the children have gone. It lies in having limited your interests while they were at home. A woman cannot meet adequately the needs of those who are nearest to her if she has no interests, no friends, no occupations of her own. Without them, she is in danger of becoming so dependent on her children for these things that she is apt to be equally dependent when they have left home. She may give them the uncomfortable feeling that she is languishing without their companionship and so make the time they can spend together an uneasy duty and not the pleasant occasion it should be.

It has always seemed important to me that women should try to develop some interests in which their whole family can share. This is valuable all around. It intensifies family solidarity. It provides the children with a nucleus of things with which they have a certain familiarity when they go out to new surroundings. And it enables the women whose children have grown up to draw on already established fields of activity when they find themselves with more time and freedom.

I think people should grow naturally with their children but be ready to let them go when the time comes. It is reassuring to know that you have given them an insight into many things which may help them develop interests of their own in the future.

I remember, when my youngest son was about fifteen, taking him on a trip to Arthurdale. This is a community in a mining region which had been established experimentally to give miners out of work a chance to work on subsistence farms.

The old saying, once a miner always a miner, has some truth in it, for one of them once told me he had trouble working in the fields—because it was so hot! At least it was always cool underground. Many of the miners, when work was again available, went back. Often their wives kept the vegetables and chickens and sometimes even a cow.

This was a made community and it was the school that tied it together. And so, when I went down to visit, there was almost always a square dance at night in the schoolhouse. My son had been around all day and had seen the little homesteads of the people. In the evening he joined in the square dance. I wondered what impression he would take away from this visit. But I asked only if he had enjoyed himself and he said "yes" with the usual uncommunicativeness of his age.

Much later I was to learn that this experience had meant something to him. One day I heard my two younger sons discussing a friend of theirs and one said to the other, "The trouble with him is that he doesn't know anything about people. He has known only one kind in his life. He should go to Arthurdale."

Unconsciously, he was saying that he had had a chance to open windows outside his own narrow circle. And I felt not only rewarded but conscious that there was safety in the kind of interests which the boys would find easily as they went through life.

The development of interests while you are bringing up your children is important to them, too. The wider their range of experience, the greater the variety of people they encounter in their home life, the farther their horizons will extend and the more hospitable to new ideas they will be as they go out into the world. And in a world like ours today, with new conditions, new concepts, new ideas confronting us at every turn, that is an essential and a vital part of education.

There should never be a vacuum. Circumstances never create a vacuum. It is hostile to life. We create vacuums for ourselves by sheer apathy. If you can manage some connection with outside things, however fleeting and remote, your new leisure will expand your opportunity to plunge into them more intensively.

A great many people fear that their interests will decrease when their children leave home. They have been devoting a number of years to caring for the young, looking after their physical needs, guiding their education, helping with their emotional problems. Now the the children are launched and, except in secondary ways, they no longer need their parents. And that is how it should be. If they still need you fundamentally, you have made them too dependent on you to face life alone. If you need them, you are too dependent.

One phase of life has ended and another has begun. Or rather, one has merged into another and broadened. You have more leisure now, more time for the organizations which you were unable to help before, for the community problems you had no time to work on, for your own talents which you may have set aside for future development.

I happen to have a niece who has great talent for drawing and sculpture but, while she wanted to be creative, she felt that nothing could be more creative than to have children, to help them grow and become useful men and women. She never completely put her talents aside but, with four strenuous children growing up, she certainly did not work hard to develop them.

But all the time she was maturing and her talents were waiting to be developed. I am sure when the opportunity does come, as it will before long, she will have much more to bring to her art than she would have had if she had been unwilling to live to the fullest extent with her children until they were ready to fly on their own.

It is true that when children have left the family environment, you are left alone but, as long as I can remember, I had a great variety of friends. I have liked to know as many different kinds of people as possible, from all possible walks of life, from all sorts of environment, from many nations and cultures.

Once, when my son Franklin was at Harvard, he went to a theater with a friend. After the performance his friend said, "Don't you want to go around to the stage door?"

"No," Franklin said. "Mummie has show girls around all the time. They're not in the least interesting."

I could see the story was funny, but I was rather pleased, too.

Among my friends were a number of trade-union people. One summer we went sailing at Campobello with some of them. One of the women told the boys about her life. It was a world they had never known and they were enthralled. Later, when someone asked one of my sons, "Who's been staying with you?" he replied, "Oh, some of Mummie's strange friends. But they are darned interesting, too."

Since everybody is an individual, nobody can be you. You are unique. No one can tell you how to use your time. It is yours. Your life is your own. You mold it. You make it. All anyone can do is to point out ways and means which have been helpful to others. Perhaps they will serve as suggestions to stimulate your own thinking until you know what it is that will fulfill you, will help you to find out what you want to do with your life.

Each of us has, as my husband's rather grim-faced ancestress pointed out, all the time there is. Those years, weeks, hours, are the sands in the glass running swiftly away. To let them drift through our fingers is tragic waste. To use them to the hilt, making them count for something, is the beginning of wisdom.

chapter 4

The Difficult Art of Maturity

A few years ago, someone asked me for my definition of a mature person. Here It Is:

"A mature person is one who does not think only in absolutes, who is able to be objective even when deeply stirred emotionally, who has learned that there is both good and bad in all people and in all things, and who walks humbly and deals charitably with the circumstances of life, knowing that in this world all of us need both love and charity."

At the time, that was the best I could do. But I have thought much about that definition since then and realize that it is not comprehensive enough to cover all the qualities that indicate the real maturity of a human personality.

First, I think, is self-knowledge. One must be willing to have knowledge of oneself. You have to be honest with yourself. You must try to understand truthfully what makes you do things or feel things. Until you have been able to face the truth about yourself you cannot be really sympathetic or understanding in regard to what happens to other people. But it takes courage to face yourself and to acknowledge what motivates you in the things you do.

This self-knowledge develops slowly. You cannot attain it all at once simply by stopping to take stock of your personal assets and liabilities. In a way, one is checked by all that protective veiling one hangs over the real motives so that it is difficult to get at the truth. But if you keep trying, honestly and courageously, even when the knowledge makes you wince, even when it shocks you and you rebel against it, it is apt to come in flashes of sudden insight. "Oh, so that is why I did that!" or "Why didn't I realize that I didn't mean that at all?" or "Now I see why I was afraid to do that!"

There is a danger in this self-examination. Some people become so interested, so fascinated, by this voyage of self-discovery, that they don't come out of it again. They remain completely absorbed in their self-study.

In my own position, I find that self-knowledge is essential in keeping a balance. Because of a variety of circumstances I have to listen to a great deal of praise. If I were to take it at its face value I would become utterly obnoxious; but, knowing myself, I realize that it is nonsense, and simply the result of a combination of circumstances.

First of all, I inherited the good will that came to my husband because he lived during a period in history in which he was given both the power and the desire to help people when they needed him. Having the qualities of leadership, he was able to give great numbers of people a new start in life. Like all leaders, he had plenty of people who hated him, but there were a great number of people who loved him, and when he died I inherited some of that good will only because of association with the things which he had done.

Then, because my interests lay along many of the same lines, and I had done some things myself in this period when people needed help, I was able to go on, and many people gave me credit for doing things which actually I could never have done alone. Much of the effectiveness I had was due to association with other people.

The knowledge of how little you can do alone teaches you humility. No matter how much adulation may come your way, once you really understand your limitations you are able to sit and listen to praise and feel quite detached, as though you were looking at the picture of someone else.

It is easy for us to be quite misled about ourselves, about our bad qualities as well as our good. And it is impossible to proceed with the right motives instead of the wrong ones as long as we have any serious misconception about ourselves.

If you have established the right motives it will help you greatly in assessing other people. You can never do this on a sound basis while you are deceived in regard to yourself. This is basic in dealing with young people. If you see your own motives clearly, you will find it much easier to lead the young to an understanding of what makes them do the things they do.

It is curious that many people seem to fear self-knowledge because they assume, and often quite wrongly, that it implies discovering only derogatory things about oneself. Actually, an important part of self-knowledge is that it gives one a better realization of the inner strength that can be called upon, of which one may be quite unaware.

Because it is easier to say, "I can't," than "I can," or at least "I can try," many people go through life unaware of untapped strength, even untapped ability. They haven't explored their own capabilities. They really don't know where their strength lies.

When I was a young girl, I was quite sure that unless someone provided me with a livelihood I would be helpless. All I could think of that I was capable of doing was to be a housemaid or a nurse to children. I did not think I could cook, because I had never done it. I had to learn by doing and I believe I would never have learned had certain things not been forced upon me.

You see this inability to make a real self-assessment quite often in other people, if not in yourself. A neighbor, perhaps, may be doggedly trying to follow some occupation that is wrong for him because, quite honestly, he is unaware of his particular strength or forte, though it may be glaringly obvious to other people.

Of course, there is always the more painful necessity of becoming aware of one's own limitations and learning to accept them. Perhaps one of the most difficult things any of us has to do is to be able to say clearly, "This is a limitation in me. Here is a case where, because of some lack of experience or some personal incapacity, I cannot meet a situation; I cannot meet the need of someone whom I dearly love, my husband or my children."

You have not sufficient experience to understand the need or you have not grown enough or you are still tied by some limitation you do not recognize and so you cannot help. I think everyone, at some time in his life, has this happen to him, comes face to face with the bitter realization that he has failed in something that means a tremendous amount and probably in a relation that is close to him.

Life teaches you that you cannot attain real maturity until you are ready to accept this harsh knowledge, this limitation in yourself, and make the difficult adjustment. Either you must learn to allow someone else to meet the need, without bitterness or envy, and accept it; or somehow you must make yourself learn to meet it. If you refuse to accept the limitation in yourself, you will be unable to grow beyond this point.

There is nothing easy about this problem, no easy way of accepting and acknowledging your limitation, no easy way of swallowing the unpalatable fact that someone else must meet the need, if you have failed. But it must be done. If you refuse to do it, you will become dishonest with yourself, making a pretense that the limitation is not there, that you have not failed. But the situation has remained unsolved and the deception fools only yourself.

There is another ingredient of the maturing process that is almost as painful as accepting your own limitations and the knowledge of what you are unable to give. That is learning to accept what other people are unable to give you. You must learn not to demand the impossible or to be upset when you do not get it.

Self-knowledge helps in this because when you understand yourself clearly it is easier for you to understand more clearly the people whom you love.

Let me give you an example of how one young woman learned to deal with a personal relationship when she had realized and faced the limitations that were involved.

Her husband forgot their wedding anniversary and the children's birthdays and she was much hurt. Then she faced the fact that his life was busy, he was engrossed in matters of great importance. If he neglected to do the things she wanted and had expected of him, it was not because he did not want to make her happy, it was because there was so much else on his mind.

She learned to handle the situation by giving him subtle reminders a few days before each anniversary, so that he would not overlook them. She would leave a casual note for him, saying, "Four days from now is our anniversary. Could we plan a little time together?" Or, if she knew he was going on a trip, she would say, "Can you change it for a few days? This is our anniversary and we like to be together."

It was never a reproof or a suggestion that he had been inadequate, but simply a reminder that this was something they would both like to remember and she just happened to have it in mind.

When she learned to understand the situation she was able to prevent the children from being upset because Daddy had forgotten. A few days before a birthday she would say casually, "Do you remember how pleasant the day was when Johnny was born?"

It was a back-handed reminder. He knew what she was doing and he was grateful.

How much worse it would have been if she had waited for the anniversary and then said, "You have forgotten that this is my birthday." This would have given him a sense of guilt and made the day unhappy for them both.

So it is a major part of maturity to accept not only your own shortcomings but those of the people you love, and help them not to fail when you can.

There is another and perhaps greater danger involved in this matter of accepting the limitations of others. Sometimes we are apt to regard as limitations qualities that are actually the other person's strength. We may resent them because they are not the particular qualities which we may want the other person to have. The danger lies in the possibility that we will not accept the person as he is but try to make him over according to our own ideas.

I think one of the basic things to recognize is that the only valuable development is the development of an individual. If you try to change that individual so that he loses his personality, you have done something that has destroyed the most important thing about a human being, his essential difference from anybody else. Any one of us who tries to make someone over and force him into an image of what we think he should be, rather than encourage him to develop along his own lines, is doing a dangerous thing.

Sooner or later, an individual will rebel if the effort is made to pour him into a mold for which he has no affinity.

True, you can sometimes stop or cripple the full development of a personality but I do not think it is ever accomplished without deep resentment on the part of the person.

I have seen parents who use sarcasm and every kind of pressure they can bring to bear to change their children and force them into the pattern of which they approve. Sometimes I have seen parents make a tremendous effort to have their children become what they themselves had wanted to be and for some reason had failed to achieve. Or they may have a great, though unacknowledged, desire to hold the child close to them and, through the child, attain a sort of continuity with the future, and know their own work will be carried on. Sometimes they succeed, but at the cost of rebellion and the actual destruction of what was essentially individual in the person.

At some point, a strong individual will usually break away and follow what he believes to be his own necessary development. But it may be only after much harm has been done and at the cost of much pain in the human relationship.

The only way in which we can really help people to develop is to let them do it themselves, trying to show them by demonstration, if we can, the things that are really needed. But to force anything upon an individual is rarely successful in helping him develop his own individuality.

Everyone should be made to feel that it is an important thing to develop his true nature. We should not compare ourselves with others, certainly we should not imitate them. I have often noticed that the person who has followed his true bent has more self-respect than the one who has been forced into an alien mold. And without self-respect, few people are able to feel genuine respect for others.

Just as we must learn to accept the limitations of others, so we must learn never to demand of someone else what is not freely offered us. This can apply to one's husband or wife, to one's children, particularly after they have left home, to one's friends. What is freely given in love or affection or companionship one should rightly rejoice in. But what is withheld one must not demand.

There are, of course, many ways of making such a demand, and the worst ways are not necessarily the overt ones, the open complaints, the querulous insistence. One can demand by implied appeals to sympathy and to duty, by pathos and helplessness and, in extreme cases, by illness.

This kind of demand is a form of spiritual blackmail and it sometimes develops into a ruthlessness, an emotional pressure which is essentially dishonest. It is not, unhappily, uncommon. People often refuse to recognize it in themselves. They regard themselves as abused, ill treated, neglected, everything, in fact, but what they are—attempting to get by force something that people are unwilling to give them. If they refuse to correct this tendency, then at least their victims must learn to resist steadily and firmly the assaults of this spiritual blackmailer.

Maturity means, too, an ability to take criticism and evaluate it. When it is not of value, when it is not constructive, but destructive, one can forget it. But when it is constructive one must accept it and try to profit, even though hurt by it. Perhaps you were hurt because a certain person pointed out a fault and you did not want that person to think you had a fault. But, if you are mature enough, you will accept the criticism of those you love and who love you and learn from it.

There is much criticism, of course, that comes to anyone who lives his life more or less before the public. Some of it may be entirely justified. Some of it, you may often feel, is unfair. In my own case, it is the criticism not of myself alone but of my husband and my family which has to be considered and evaluated and accepted.

If you consider that you are being criticized by someone who is seeking knowledge and has an open mind, then you naturally feel you must try to meet that criticism, that you must try to make an explanation, which may or may not satisfy the critic. But if you feel that the criticism is made out of sheer malice and that no amount of explanation will change a point of view which has nothing to do with the facts, then the best thing is to put it out of your mind entirely, as though it did not touch you or your loved ones in any way.

For some people this is hard to do. In fact, I know some for whom it is impossible. But I find that you can close the door and turn to other things, knowing that nothing can be achieved by giving any further attention to it.

Another sign of maturity is gradually to eliminate the faults you see in yourself but that no one else knows exist. If no one else is conscious of a failing we have, a great many of us are apt to hide it instead of trying to eliminate it. We are glossing over something instead of honestly trying to get rid of it. Saying to yourself, "Well, after all, nobody knows," is no solution. Because you know.

Maturity also means that you have set your values, that you know what you really want out of life. What are the things that give you great satisfaction? I know my satisfaction is not in politics, not in the interesting things I do. It is in being with people I am fond of and feeling that in some small way I can make life happier or more interesting for them, or help them to achieve their objective. To me that is much more important than anything else in my life.

To be mature you have to realize what you value most. It is extraordinary to discover that comparatively few people reach this level of maturity. They seem never to have paused to consider what has value *for them*. They spend great effort and sometimes make great sacrifices for values that, fundamentally, meet no real needs of their own. Perhaps they have imbibed the values of their particular profession or job, of their community or their neighbors, of their parents or family. Not to arrive at a clear understanding of one's own values is a tragic waste. You have missed the whole point of what life is for.

chapter 5

Readjustment Is Endless

Women have one advantage over men. Throughout history they have been forced to make adjustments. They have adapted their own personal wishes and ambitions and hopes to those of their husbands, their children, and the requirements of their homes. In the great majority, they have arranged to fit their own interests into a pattern primarily concerned with the interests of others. This has not always been an easy process but the result is that, in most cases, it is less difficult for a woman to adjust to new situations than it is for a man.

From the time they are little girls women are expected to adapt themselves. They do this first in learning how to manage their father; then it is only a step to knowing how to manage their young men, and finally their husbands. But it is always the woman who is making the chief adjustment, finding how to behave in order to get what she wants, and also to give what she has to give.

There are few cases in which women do not accept the fact that their homes must be run to suit their husband's needs and wishes, in which they do not adjust to the way of life of the man with whom they now have life's closest relationship.

The man, on the other hand, often grows up with the idea that he should be able to dominate the forces of nature, the forces of his material world. He seeks to make them adjust to him. It is one reason why men tend to be more conservative than women. In business, they are apt to fight against new things unless they have initiated them. They do not want to make this adjustment.

The result of these two conflicting types of training is that women today appear to be able to adjust themselves to the conditions and the concepts of a changing world more easily than men.

Readjustment is a kind of private revolution. Each time you learn something new you must readjust the whole framework of your knowledge. It seems to me that one is forced to make inner and outer readjustments all one's life. The process never ends. And yet, for a great many people, this is a continuing problem because they appear to have an innate fear of change, no matter what form it takes: changed personal relationships, changed social or financial conditions. The new or the unknown becomes in their minds something hostile, almost malignant.

It is not only in times of great world changes like the present that readjustment is necessary, though it is certainly more vital now. No matter how outwardly tranquil or unchanging one's situation may appear to be, it requires constant readjustment.

Let's start with the most obvious and inescapable part of adjustment, the changes, physical and emotional, that are an inherent part of every stage of growth and aging. Almost everyone recognizes this necessity for readjustment during the period of adolescence, but we do not seem to be equally aware of it in terms of middle age, of the elderly, of the old.

Every age, someone has said, is an undiscovered country. We are constantly advancing, like explorers, into the unknown, which makes life an adventure all the way. How interminable and dull that journey would be if it were on a straight road over a flat plain, if we could see ahead the whole distance, without surprises, without the salt of the unexpected, without challenge. I wish with all my heart that every child could be so imbued with a sense of the adventure of life that each change, each readjustment, each surprise—good or bad—that came along would be welcomed as a part of the whole enthralling experience.

Today, the adolescent gets a disproportionate amount of attention. Adolescence is often a trying period but certainly it is no more difficult than any other part of the aging process. True, there are physical and emotional changes. But middle age, too, has its physical and emotional changes. So does old age. Youth has an immense advantage here, which is too often overlooked in self-pity. The bodily and emotional changes are revelations of development, an awareness of a wider scope of power. But the changes that come in the middle and later

years are an indication of the decline of one's power, of deterioration. You were accustomed to doing certain things. Suddenly you discover that you can't do them any more. This, I
think, is a harder situation to meet and to meet gracefully.
Sometimes, indeed, the discovery of this deterioration of
one's powers can be a psychological shock.

There is always, of course, a great deal of comment about
middle-aged women and their problems in meeting the physical and mental and emotional problems of the menopause. But
I am inclined to believe that for men the aging process is more
painful than for women, who learned so young to adjust. For
a man who has been accustomed to have people dependent on
him, the decline of the period of dominance, the approach of
the period of dependence, is a hard situation to face.

Whenever people talk about "the best years of a woman's life"
I feel at a loss. Some women believe that the years when their
children were small were the best years of their lives, others
the time when the children were old enough to go to school
and they were freer and could have more social life.

I enjoyed the years when my children were small, and I
have never been without plenty of social life, but I am not
sure that I always enjoyed it, because those were the years
when I was trying to get over an inferiority complex as far as
formal social life was concerned. I loved my intimate friends,
but when it came to Washington dinner parties and dances,
in the days when my husband was Assistant Secretary of the
Navy, I can remember instances that are funny now but were
serious to me at the time.

I remember one party when my husband was having a good time while I was miserable. I felt that no one would really know the difference if I were not at the party at all. I slipped by my husband and said in a whisper, "I am going home. Stay here and enjoy yourself. I will see you later."

I forgot to ask for the key to the front door. I took a taxi and went home. Then I found I had no key. We had an outer and an inner door, so I moved the mat close to the wall and, in my evening dress, I sat for three solid hours, waiting for my husband, feeling sorry for myself because he had not left his good time to come with me, although I had not given him the opportunity to make the choice. When you know you have no justification for self-pity and you want to pity yourself it is much worse than if you have a real grievance.

When my husband finally did come home and let me in the house I don't remember whether I was a disagreeable or a pleasant companion, but I am quite sure I made him feel guilty by the mere fact of having waited there.

I am convinced that those years, which I suppose many people would feel should have been the best years of my life, were actually not the best.

Whatever period of life we are in is good only to the extent that we make use of it, that we live it to the hilt, that we continue to develop and understand what it has to offer us and we have to offer it. The rewards for each age are different in kind, but they are not necessarily different in value or in satisfaction.

People develop at different ages and overcome things at different times, so you cannot expect that everyone will feel that the most rewarding years of their lives came during the time of youth. It may well be that one's development came later and therefore one will feel the results at a later period.

To be unable, because of inflexibility, to readjust to changes will result in a kind of sterility, great unhappiness, and sometimes almost a state of shock.

When my mother-in-law died in 1941, my husband said something I have never forgotten. He said that, though he missed his mother, he was consoled for her death in one way because she would have found it too difficult to readjust to a way of life she had not always known. She could not have faced seeing her grandsons go off to war, she could not have reconciled herself to the fact that it was no longer possible for anyone to maintain a household on the scale to which she had been accustomed all her life.

And yet I have known many cases where, because people had been able to adjust to changing conditions as they went along, they were able to make huge readjustments when it became necessary.

One reason for this ability to cope with disaster is that *nothing ever happens to us except what happens in our minds.* Unhappiness is an inward, not an outward, thing. It is as independent of circumstances as is happiness. Consider the truly happy people you know. I think it is unlikely that you will find that circumstances have made them happy. They have made themselves happy in spite of circumstances.

A case that comes most pressingly to my mind is that of my friend, Miss Hickok. For many years she was an Associated Press reporter and later an investigator for Harry

Hopkins. Always she lived a dynamic life, surrounded by the-
atrical and political people, her friends among the celebrities
in half a dozen fields, the news of the day a part of the very
fabric of her life.

Then the unexpected, the unforeseen, happened to her as
it has to so many others. She developed a crippling arthritis
and diabetes, which finally affected her eyes. The activities
that had made up her life were no longer possible. How was
she going to live in the future?

I suggested that she come up to Hyde Park and try to
write. After a few months, she moved to a little cabin of her
own and plunged into the writing of children's books. She
could type only with one hand. She could work only one
hour at a time because of her eyes. She could no longer read a
newspaper nor could she watch television. There had been a
time when not reading a paper would have seemed like death
itself.

But Hick took her limitations in her stride. By listening to
the radio she has become much better informed on the news
and the course of events than most people. She was a big-city
woman but she has become friends with the neighborhood
women of a small village. The children from the vicinity
began to seek her out and to listen to her stories. She has taken
what seemed to be a disaster, made her difficult adjustment,
and created a new life, among new people, doing new work.

It could not have been this kind of triumph if she had not,
to begin with, had a real interest in people, an interest which
was not limited to one kind of people. She had the courage to
meet discouragement and turn defeat into a victory. People

can surmount what seems to be total defeat, difficulties too great to be borne, but it requires a capacity to readjust endlessly to the changing conditions of life.

Like countless other women, I had to face the future alone after the death of my husband, making the adjustment to being by myself, to planning without someone else as the center of my world. Long before, of course, I had learned that the process of readjustment never stops.

Many readjustments that I have made I did not particularly want to make, but they were required by circumstances. In planning the future, on my own, I had to make sure that this largest readjustment of all would meet, as far as possible, what I honestly felt I wanted out of life.

I met, as so many women have met, the loneliness that can be so devastating, if one permits it to be, when there is no longer an emotional center to one's life. But I discovered that by keeping as busy as possible I could manage increasingly to keep my loneliness at bay. The advantage of being busy is that you don't have time to think about yourself.

I have always felt that I was particularly fortunate because, for many years, I had had a very warm relationship with my secretary, Miss Malvina Thompson. She had worked for me in New York both when I was associated with Miss Dickerman's school and later when I was a member of the Democratic State Committee. She decided to go to Washington when we went there. She lived in her own apartment and she had her own life but we grew very close.

One summer, at Hyde Park, I settled her in a cottage a few

miles back from the river where I live today. She had her own apartment and I went over there to work, as we had made the discovery that if we mixed my mail and that of my husband, the task of disentangling it was beyond anyone's ability.

Without realizing it, Miss Thompson was becoming not only a part of my life but of the entire family. The grand-children would run to her for advice and sympathy. My own children would ask her to do things for them. And so, when we left the White House and came back to New York, she took an apartment in the same house where I had taken one. After a little while we decided that she should move to my apartment as I had more room than was necessary.

She kept her own apartment at the cottage in Hyde Park, but I used the rest of the house. Actually, we were living to-gether, making no demands on each other—at least, she never made any demand on me. We lived our own lives, but she was always there. It makes a great difference not to come back to an empty house. I realize that the reason I adjusted so easily to loneliness was probably due in large part to the background of a warm relationship with Tommy, as all of us called her.

When she died, I learned for the first time what being alone was like, but the interim had made the transition easier and also I was older. Somehow, with age, closing a door and being alone is perhaps not quite as difficult, though you may still not always find it pleasant.

As I look back, I think of my own grandmother, who made some of the biggest adjustments I ever saw a human being make. I came to the conclusion that she was able to

make them partly because, with advancing age, you accept
the blows of life more philosophically. In fact, you accept
life, which is perhaps nature's way of preparing you to accept death. It seems to me that when people grow old, death
gradually becomes part of the natural scheme of life. Death
is unnatural when it comes to the young, but with age it is
normal and inevitable and, like everything else that has been
inevitable in life, becomes easier to accept.

Some people have certain religious beliefs which they
find help them to meet death with greater equanimity.
I happen to think that a belief in God is really all that is
necessary for the acceptance of death, since you know that
death, like life, is part of God's pattern. Nature makes it easier if you are old, and if you have matured in a way to accept
life and death as part of God's pattern, as you accept the
changing seasons.

One of the things that changes most with living is one's personal relationships, especially if one must move to different
places, as so many Americans do. One's immediate family relations will remain intact, but one's links with one's friends
are in danger of being broken. And yet, even if there is no
problem of distance involved, one must make a continuing
effort to keep personal relationships warm and close, in the
family as well as among friends. Human relationships, like
life itself, can never remain static. They grow or they dimin-
ish. But, in either case, they change. Our emotional interests,
our intellectual pursuits, our personal preoccupations, all
change. So do those of our friends. So the relationship that

binds us together must change too; it must be flexible enough to meet the alterations of person and circumstance.

To be able to build new relations is as important as to hold the old ones, though sometimes one is obliged to sever old relationships for a great variety of reasons. I have seen one person obliged to do this because of a drastically altered financial situation. If she had not been able to develop new relations and interests this would have been a hard change to undergo. As it is, the change has been made with comparative ease.

No relationship in this world ever remains warm and close unless a real effort is made on both sides to keep it so. You can even slip away from your children if you do not take a tremendous amount of trouble to find out what is happening to them and to keep the warmth, the closeness, alive.

One of the things that is often held against American businessmen is that they get so wrapped up in business or just in making money that they neglect to cultivate relations at home and with outside friends.

I don't think the American businessman often realizes that he sometimes separates his business life so completely from his home life that he ceases to make a partner of his wife, who knows nothing of what occupies him during the day. He may often subconsciously resent this, but he does nothing to change it. Then she becomes immersed in the children and is resentful because he is not enough interested in them.

Many of us have known American businessmen who were hurrying to make a fortune so that they could enjoy life. But "making a fortune" is a flexible thing; what seemed a fortune to you at one point may not seem even adequate at another. So you are apt to keep on and on, forgetting that while you try to make the wherewithal to give you leisure, you are neglecting to learn how to use the leisure when you have it.

Often these men who work for their wives and their children deny their children the most precious thing they can give them, a close companionship. A companionship with your child must be built. It does not just happen. A man requires considerable thought and effort to develop the right kind of companionship with sons, and a different kind with daughters.

Daughters will be grateful and remember all their lives the things which their fathers introduced them to: gentleness and thoughtfulness and appreciation of themselves as women. These are qualities which, someday, they will look for in their maturity.

I still remember the first day my father invited me, as he would a young lady, to lunch with him. When he came to get me—I was only seven—he brought me a small bouquet, which he himself pinned on. With what pride I walked that day, and how I kept those flowers!

One of the most drastic readjustments was forced during the second quarter of this century on millions of people, uprooted by war, their homes, their very countries gone, perhaps their families scattered over the face of the earth, never to meet again.

Some of the men and women who have been driven from their lands because of prejudice and political reasons and have taken refuge here have a new kind of readjustment to make.

I know a doctor who came here with his wife, almost penniless, not knowing English, and unable to practice medicine until he had complied with the requirements of this country. First he had to learn the language and then retake the medical examinations. Meanwhile, he had to live. He and his wife found jobs as domestic servants, working as butler and cook, with the arrangement that he would have time off to study.

Then they had to think of something they could do so that he could afford to go to college. They opened a candy shop, made excellent candy, and did well selling it.

He went to college, got his license, and settled in a country district; he felt that he would be needed there as the only doctor was very old. Before long he was known and recognized throughout the whole community, and today he is successful.

Most middle-aged people would quail at the thought of making such an adjustment. There are always a few who succumb to despair. To start all over! To begin again at the beginning! But for those two people the adjustment was possible because they were mature. They were sure of their own position; they did not feel that being servants lowered them. They kept their dignity and worked hard. That, of course, was part of the dignity. Nor were they in the least embarrassed by their altered status. There was a sound reason for it.

When they went out, they visited their friends on quite a different basis. I was always amused by the picture of what would happen if they were to meet socially the people whom they had served. Fortunately for them they did not suffer from that crippling false shame which hampers so many people who, feeling insecure, are driven to assert too much.

There are many people of mature age who are making this kind of major readjustment after having attained a place and profession in their own country and acquired substantial means. Stripped of their possessions and their money, they must start once more at the beginning. They must re-educate themselves, first in the language and second in the new customs. They must re-train themselves in the profession, which, in their own country, they had already mastered. To an older man, this is irksome, but in order to comform to the law and have an opportunity to start life once again, it must be done.

It has always seemed to me that, with the exception of mastering a new language, this is the same sort of experience which many people have to face when they have reached the age for retirement in so many businesses and professions. For a long time I have felt that our old-age retirement provisions are quite wrong. Each case should be judged on its own merits. Many people are as vigorous at sixty-five as they were at forty-five, with the added advantage of years of experience. Yet they often face compulsory retirement.

If such people are wise they may arrange to go somewhere else, where their past experience is appreciated and where they can exercise the same profession. For them, too, this may mean acquiring a new language or adapting the knowledge and experience they have gained to a new profession.

Enforced retirement can be a serious situation for doctors who are still vigorous and have held a hospital position for many years. It must be terrible for them to face. If they have been wise they will build, during the last years before retirement, an independent practice. In these circumstances, they can regulate, to suit their own needs, the hours they spend working. They can continue to feel that the profession to which they have dedicated their lives is still being served and that the community is not losing the services for which they were trained.

Aside from the waste of human ability, training, and experience that comes through forced retirement, in many cases there is a definite loss to the community which needs now, as always, all the ability it can get. I remember one government expert on food who was asked to go to South America to develop the use of new foods. Though he had been retired, he was able to put in a good many years of valuable service, even after going back to school to learn the language of the country in which he was to work.

We should think more of ways in which we can use our retired people and the mature people who come to this country. We should give some recognition to the skills they can bring us. The sooner they are able to use their capabilities, the sooner we will benefit by them in this country. We are allowing waste in our most valuable material, our human resources.

Because science has lengthened the span of life for so many people it is necessary that we give older people an opportunity to be useful and productive. Otherwise we put on people in the middle stream of life, between the protected years of youth and old age, too great a burden. They have to provide the wherewithal to protect youth and prepare the young to take up the burden of the middle years. They also have to provide, in one way and another, for an increasing number of older people.

The present situation has reached a kind of stalemate. Older people are retired to make room for the younger ones, with a result that the younger ones must look after them. We are guilty of great waste because of a groundless and point-less fear.

For many generations there was no particular change in the family income. From father to son the situation remained approximately the same. But wars, depressions, and the—perhaps I could call it the invisible—revolution in the United States have all had their effect on income.

As young people advance in their jobs and earn more money, they have an important and difficult adjustment to make. They must learn the best ways in which to use this larger income. Will they have more education? Will they add certain things to their homes they never thought of having, such as music or pictures? Will they have more service? They must make the decisions.

I am interested in this because it means primarily an ad-justment of one's sense of values. A nation like ours, where changes are continual, must be particularly careful about how it makes these adjustments. If people come up the fi-nancial ladder but still maintain a low educational standard, with its lack of appreciation of many of the things of artistic and spiritual value, the nation will not be able to grow to its real stature.

This is a challenge which the Soviet government has met effectively. In the past, education was denied to the great bulk of the people. Today, it is one of the greatest gains they have made. Education is not only available to the people, it is highly respected. The ownership of books is a token of moving up the social as well as the cultural ladder. Intellectual attainments and a developing culture are the road to better and richer living.

While the Russians are straining to deepen and broaden and extend their cultural and intellectual horizon, we cannot afford to be indifferent and to neglect our own development.

chapter 6

Learning to Be Useful

Happiness is not a goal, it is a by-product. Paradoxically, the one sure way not to be happy is deliberately to map out a way of life in which one would please oneself completely and exclusively. After a short time, a very short time, there would be little that one really enjoyed. For what keeps our interest in life and makes us look forward to tomorrow is giving pleasure to other people.

When I found myself alone I might, quite easily, have decided that I would give up my usual activities, that from then on I was going to do only what I really wanted for my own pleasure. Perhaps, in the beginning, my family and my friends and my associates would have been shocked. But in a very little while they would have accepted the changed situation, my place would have been filled by others, and I myself would have been forgotten and, worse, unneeded.

It is easy to slip into self-absorption and it is equally fatal. When one becomes absorbed in himself, in his health, in his personal problems, or in the small details of daily living, he is, at the same time, losing interest in other people; worse, he is losing his ties to life. From that it is an easy step to losing interest in the world and in life itself. That is the beginning of death.

I have always liked Don Quixote's comment, "Until death it is all life."

Someone once asked me what I regarded as the three most important requirements for happiness. My answer was: "A feeling that you have been honest with yourself and those around you; a feeling that you have done the best you could both in your personal life and in your work; and the ability to love others."

But there is another basic requirement, and I can't understand now how I forgot it at the time: that is the feeling that you are, in some way, useful. Usefulness, whatever form it may take, is the price we should pay for the air we breathe and the food we eat and the privilege of being alive. And it is its own reward, as well, for it is the beginning of happiness, just as self-pity and withdrawal from the battle are the beginning of misery.

When I was a young girl I lived for several years with a cousin of my mother's. Because she was not as pretty as my mother and my aunts, she had developed an inferiority complex. Then she married a gentle and kindly man who gave her all the feeling of importance she needed; sheltered her from all unpleasantness; made, as few men do, the adjustments in his own wishes to meet hers. Like most rich people of the time, she knew many distinguished people and served on boards and led a highly satisfactory life.

Then she began to lose her friends, as we all do when we grow older. Her husband died and she had less money than she had been accustomed to. She was also deprived of his unremitting attention and care. She could not endure the change. She would not adjust to it. What she wanted, with quiet stubbornness, was to return to the life that was gone.

In order to achieve her goal she became an invalid, she made herself a completely helpless person so that she could command the attention that was no longer freely given.

For two years I lived in her house—indeed, I was married from it—and though I am grateful to her for that, I remember, too, that I, like everyone within her range, conformed to her needs, to her wishes, to her comfort. Even after my husband became President of the United States and my duties multiplied, I could see her, on my rapid visits to New York, only at the hours that suited her own convenience.

She was well to do, there was nothing really wrong with her health, she had the world to explore. But she lay in bed, growing more and more sorry for herself, more and more self-indulgent. Self-pity hung like a fog in the room with her. Now and then, she would say wistfully that she longed to go to a concert or visit a museum. But, of course, that was impossible for her.

Once I had the temerity to send in a doctor who examined her and listened to her complaints. She told him of her hopeless wish to hear music and to see fine paintings again.

"There is no reason on earth why you can't do it," he told her bluntly.

She resented him deeply and refused ever to see him again. She had found a way of forcing life to give her what she wanted and she would not change. The only trouble was that it brought no happiness with it.

Actually, she had the mentality which, had she developed it, would have enabled her to do a great many things. She could have been a good executive. She might have developed talents of many kinds. But what she wanted most was the power to make others answer her wishes. When she found that it was hard work to obtain the power by doing something that required real effort and development on her part, she accepted the easier way of gaining power through being an invalid. She made use of the terrible strength which is weakness. She wanted happiness, but her method of seeking it defeated her.

I think everyone, from the earliest possible age, should be taught not to be sorry for himself; not, whatever the provocation, whatever the temptation, to carry his depression or his disappointments or his black moods to someone else.

I remember with some amusement a small child who lived for a time at the White House. He was frail and timid and given to tears. One day I said firmly, "Nobody likes people who cry. If you are happy everyone will want to be with you. If you are sad and cry, nobody will want to be with you. If you must cry, go into the bathroom and cry alone into the bathtub."

A few days later, I was going through the hallway and saw the small three-year-old crying his heart out, curled up in a big leather chair outside my husband's room.

I looked my reproach, but before I had a chance to say anything he wailed, "I can't find a bathtub to cry into alone. He's in there!"

For each of us our load of trouble is our personal burden to carry, not something to be sloughed off on someone else. Also, and it's a curious thing, if you don't make a parade of your unhappiness to someone else, you'll find it is a lot easier to get over it.

Most women, I have already said, learn early in life to make adjustments of their own wishes and plans to meet the needs of others. But most women, I think, though they may complain a little about this, would agree that meeting the needs of others is not a real burden; it is what makes life worth living. It is probably the deepest satisfaction a woman has.

The need to be needed is much stronger in most of us than we are aware. We hear a great deal about the need for self-expression but, by and large, it rarely brings the same returns in basic satisfaction that come with going beyond the self to meet another person's need.

One reason why we sometimes find less delinquency proportionately among the poor is that the children have a greater sense of being needed in the family. They have a sense of belonging, of shared responsibility, of being an essential—and necessary—part of a component whole. Often I hear people exclaim in surprise when they come across cases of delinquency in young people who are accustomed to a high standard of living and have everything, presumably, to make life worth while. And to make it easy. Why, they ask, are these youngsters, who have so much, antisocial in their behavior?

The answer seems to be that however attractive the home surroundings may be, the parents have not made the child feel necessary to the home life, a really vital part of all the projects and planning of home existence. In some ways, this situation has been bettered with the gradual disappearance of personal service in the homes of all but the very wealthy. The children have learned that they must carry their share of the work around the house and this has made them feel that they are truly a part of it, and especially, a *needed* part.

There is in every child a strong need for the love of others and for identification as an individual. This was borne in upon me sharply this summer. Every year I give a picnic for a group of delinquent children; the majority are colored children, a few are little white boys who have already been rejected by other groups dealing with delinquent cases, so these are exceptionally difficult youngsters.

During the last picnic a small white boy came up and clutched at my hand. "Do you remember me?"

I did, of course, and I said so, for I had seen him on several other occasions.

"What's my name?" he asked me anxiously.

I couldn't tell him. I had seen so many children on so many occasions during the year that I could not possibly remember all their names. I tried to explain.

He watched me sharply. Then he told me his name.

A few minutes later he appeared at my side again. "What's my name?" he demanded. And this time I was able to tell him. He brightened.

A third time he came back. "What's my name?" When I answered correctly he nodded with satisfaction. "I guess now you'll know who I am," he said.

That desperate need for identification and recognition as an individual comes up all through life to people who, because of circumstances or some limitation in themselves, have not learned to feel that they have developed as individuals or have been so accepted.

Not long ago there was much surprise over a newspaper item which pointed out that rural parts of northern Italy had the lowest delinquency ratio in the Western world. It couldn't possibly be true, someone said. The ratio was much higher in this country for the same people.

But the situation, of course, was entirely different. In northern Italy large families live and work together in farming the land. They are all necessary to the welfare of the group as a whole. They are responsible for it, and have mutual respect and mutual dependence. But when they come to the United States, it frequently happens that the parents fail to learn the language as quickly as the children.

Usually these immigrants seek a neighborhood or an occupation where they can be with people who speak their own tongue and eat the same kinds of food and understand their ways. The children, on the other hand, are in school with other youngsters who speak English and initiate them into American customs. With a child's need to belong, the youngsters quickly adopt these new customs, while the parents, often suspicious of innovation, cling to their own ways.

As a result, the child is often ashamed of his parents and

feels that they represent a discarded, outmoded way of life. They lose respect for them and for their authority and they refuse to accept home discipline. What makes the difference in the statistics for delinquency is the impact of different conditions and the loss of respect for parental authority.

Usefulness, to my mind, is a kind of blanket word that covers all the many kinds of service to one's fellow men. It is an expression of human love. Or, instead of love, perhaps the better word would be respect. That, I think, is a noble word, an indication of a certain attitude toward one's fellow men. Used too often in a subservient sense, it is more properly a token of equality. To respect one's fellow men is perhaps more difficult than to "love" them in a wide, vague sense. In fact, it is possible that to feel respect for mankind is better than to feel love for it. Love can often be misguided and do as much harm as good, but respect can do only good. It assumes that the other person's stature is as large as one's own, his rights as reasonable, his needs as important.

We discover this soon in dealing with children. A spoiled child will tease and be unreasonable in his attempt to get something he wants. He will also, as a rule, be unhappy. But a child who has been treated with real respect, who has a feeling that his elders expect certain standards even from a young member of the family, will behave with astonishing maturity. A child who feels the basic acceptance that goes with respect, and knows he is trusted because he is accepted, will achieve remarkable ability in acquiring self-control and consideration for others.

I had an example this summer when one of my grand-daughters proceeded to organize the picnic which I give every year for 160 people. She had watched her mother do the work at these picnics for some years and had helped. This year she organized her own age group to take charge. The grown-ups could have disappeared and the picnic would still have been given in a successful and orderly manner. Every-one would have passed along the line and had his plate filled just as well. It was all done with such quiet confidence that I stood in amazement and gave her the respect which meant a great deal more than the mere affection which she could have taken for granted. This respect had been earned.

To be useful is, in a way, to justify one's own existence. The difficult thing, perhaps, is to learn *how* to be useful, to recognize needs and to attempt to meet them.

Most people encounter this need first in the family group where, if the family is really a closely knit unit, they learn to carry their share of the responsibility for the fam-ily. They meet it next in the most difficult relationship of all, marriage, where each must learn for himself to under-stand his partner, to know what his needs are, and to meet them with unselfishness and flexibility.

They meet it next when they discover that their home is part of a community and that community a part of a larger society whose limits are increasingly wide. Someday, per-haps, they will be world-wide.

The needs of that community, of that society, are endless, beyond calculation. If you can learn to see where they are, you will find, at the same time, a way to be useful.

When I was quite young I did some work for the Consumers League. One of the things they asked me to do was to investigate the sweatshops in which artificial feathers and flowers were being made.

I was appalled. In those days, these people often worked at home, and I felt I had no right to invade their private dwellings, to ask questions, to investigate conditions. I was frightened to death.

But this was what had been required of me and I wanted to be useful. I entered my first sweatshop and walked up the steps of my first tenement. It is hard to look back and remember the terrible world that, in actual years, is not really so long ago, but was so different from the conditions we know now. I saw little children of four or five sitting at tables until they dropped with fatigue, and earning tragically little a week.

Conditions of employment were such that the workers were often in real physical danger and yet the average person was rarely aware of the situation. It took the tragedy of the Triangle fire to insure the future safety of girls working in certain establishments.

During my first year of this work I also taught a small group of children in a settlement house. Mainly this was an attempt to keep them off the streets of New York for certain hours of the day. On one occasion, a little girl was ill and Franklin, who had come to meet me, accompanied me to the tenement in which she lived. When we got out on the street afterward he drew a long breath of air. Not fresh air, there in those crowded, smelly streets with pushcarts at the curb. But better than the air in that tenement.

"My God," he said, aghast. "I didn't know people lived like that!"

But nothing could be done, of course, until someone knew the facts: seeking for them, checking them, investigating to make sure of what was actually happening. All this was necessary before anything could be done to better conditions. Until someone cared to be useful, people continued to live like that.

There are, of course, in any community, a thousand and one ways to make oneself useful. For instance, in the big city of New York I know some people who devote a definite amount of time to reading books for the blind. This can be done by anyone who will take the trouble to read accurately and with understanding of what he is reading. And it adds enormously to the pleasure of blind people who, even if they do not know Braille, can now enjoy listening to books which otherwise, unless they could afford to pay someone to read, would remain closed to them.

If you have any talents there are many ways in which you can add to other people's enjoyment. You may think that your gifts as an entertainer are primarily useful because they earn your living, but I wish I could have taken you along last year when Harry Belafonte went with me to entertain the hundred or more little delinquent boys who are at school on the other side of the river from where I live, and who are my friends because I see them every now and then. They have so few friends that even a casual visitor is regarded as an intimate.

I talk a great deal about them, for these little people are

very much on my mind. When Harry Belafonte said he would go over one afternoon with his accompanist and give them an entertainment I was delighted. What excitement for them to have someone whose name and recordings they knew well. Many of them were of the same race and they looked up to his achievements, success, and fame almost as though he were a medieval knight in armor to whom they could turn for protection.

We arrived and they swarmed around him. He gave them a performance that was even better than the one I had heard at the Waldorf. They responded with great warmth and when it was over they hung about him, asking for an autograph, asking for a word that they could treasure as their own. He gave them with equal warmth and patience.

The next afternoon I again saw him give of himself in the same way, though without the entertainment. Moving among the hospitalized children at Blythedale, New York, making their eyes shine and their faces light with smiles because he gave them an autograph, gave them a word of encouragement. For a moment the braces or the cradle in which they lay was forgotten. They were well in their bodies because he satisfied their little souls.

These are some of the ways in which you could make your talents useful. But if you have no talent, if you are just a person like myself, ask almost any charitable organization if they can use someone to fold literature and lick stamps. They will gladly accept a volunteer who can be counted on to do what he agrees to do and does it as though it were a professional job, as though he were being paid for it.

I know a man who, after working all day, gave two evenings a week to a veterans' hospital in his neighborhood. It could not have been easy to relinquish so large a part of his time for relaxation, but he did it faithfully because he had agreed to. He wheeled patients around, turned on their radios, talked to them, helped them in little but vital ways. When he moved to another town he was deeply missed because he had been faithful and never disappointed in his job.

For this is the worst part of the rather casual desire to be useful. A person sees something that should be done and offers to do it. As time passes, he becomes bored and loses interest; he becomes slack, fails to appear when he had promised to do so, fails to accomplish what he had pledged to do. This kind of amateur "helper" is perhaps more prevalent than one would wish. If you promise to perform something for the good of an individual or an organization or a community, try your best to live up to your word. For you are needed. Desperately.

I know of some boys who discovered that in their neighborhood there was a young family which could not afford to pay for professional baby sitters. They made friends and offered to do their homework in the young couple's house in the evenings so that they could have a little freedom. They said, "We can sit in your living room as well as in ours. It will be quiet and we can study. If you will just give us some supper or let us raid the icebox that will be pay enough."

I doubt if the boys knew how much it meant. The young couple whom they were helping were often tired because they were trying to learn and earn at the same time. They rarely got out of the house and away from their obligations even for a short while.

Charitable organizations and hospitals, poverty and pain—these exist, alas, everywhere. Their needs are enormous, beyond calculation. But there are others, less dramatic though no less real. There is loneliness within reach of your outstretched arm; there is unhappiness that requires, perhaps, only understanding and a fortifying word; there is hunger and sickness and despair somewhere in your neighborhood.

It has always seemed to me a great pity that man's noblest instincts, his heroic self-sacrifice, his capacity to unite with his neighbor in a common cause, emerge only in times of disaster, such as war and fire and flood. Several years ago there was a typical morning subway rush in New York. People pulled and pushed and fought their way onto the crowded train. They were heedless of each other, every man fighting for himself, set only on wedging himself into the tight-packed mob.

Then there was a cry of pain. A girl had slipped; one leg had become pinned between the train and the platform. Almost without words the men united in an effort to throw their weight against the train, pushing the car back to allow the girl to be released. Together they freed her, pulled her out, made sure that she was safe.

Then? Then as one man they hurled themselves into the train, pushing, pulling, shoving, each man for himself. Yet for a few heightened moments, at least, they had worked together for a common goal.

chapter 7

The Right to Be an Individual

We are facing a great danger today—the loss of our individuality. It is besieged on all sides by pressures to conform: to a standardized way of living, to recognized—or required—codes of behavior, to rubber-stamp thinking. But the worst threat comes from within, from a man's or woman's apathy, his willingness to surrender to pressure, to "do it the easy way," to give up the one thing that is himself, his value and his meaning as a person—his individuality.

It's your life—but only if you make it so. The standards by which you live must be your own standards, your own values, your own convictions in regard to what is right and wrong, what is true and false, what is important and what is trivial. When you adopt the standards and the values of someone else or a community or a pressure group, you surrender your own integrity. You become, to the extent of your surrender, less of a human being.

Over the years, I have had to give a great deal of thought to this whole problem of conforming and nonconforming, to determining when I should conform, when I should not. Because circumstances brought a fierce and inescapable light of publicity on any actions or words of mine, which in another person might have passed unnoticed, I had to face the fact that even trivial actions and careless words could, under that bright light, appear larger than life-size.

I remember one horrible experience at a time when the newspapers were filled with the tragedy that came to the young Lindberghs after their child was kidnaped. The whole country was roused to sympathy for them and to antagonism toward any human being who could seize upon a helpless baby and put his parents through this terrible ordeal. Rumors and stories were constantly in the papers.

I traveled up from Washington and as I came off the train in New York several reporters met me with the latest rumor that the guilty man had been found. They asked me the inevitable question: Didn't I feel that this man should go to the chair?

I had no time to reflect upon the state of public opinion or the ways that newspapers might represent or misrepresent whatever I said. So I said what I felt: namely, that I didn't think anyone should take a life when, by doing so, no good could be accomplished. If a man was innocent, as might someday be proved, then justice had miscarried. If he was guilty, you could not bring back the lost child, nor could the hours of agony which his parents had had to live through be wiped out, nor could you alleviate the suffering which they would still have to undergo.

I felt that anyone who had committed this particular type of crime was probably mentally ill. I was convinced that he should be prevented from ever again endangering his fellow human beings, but something in me has always been opposed to capital punishment. What right has one group of human beings to take away the life of any other human being? They must try him, of course, and, if the evidence warrants, see that the public is protected from any recurrence of the danger. But capital punishment seemed as wrong to me then as it does now, and I said so.

Oh, what a hornet's nest I brought down upon my head! The wife of the President had said a terrible thing, that a man should not be executed for this most dreadful crime. I was not then as accustomed to letting the adverse winds blow out as I am today, and I was horribly worried. Would what I had said harm my husband in some way?

No real harm was done and I learned again the lesson that you fear in apprehension far more than you actually suffer in reality. But I had to consider that, because of the prominence given them, my statements could hamper my husband in work that was far more important than mine could be. So I have had to weigh most carefully this major problem. If I have made mistakes of judgment, as of course I have, they have not, at least, been a result of not thinking about the whole dilemma.

It is not a new one, of course. From the beginning of time, there have been pressures on men to conform. At first, probably, there was pressure to conform to the taboos of a tribe, later to a church or to the autocratic government. But the outer pressures have always been more or less balanced by an innate drive in human beings to find and be themselves, to develop their whole natures, to make their lives an expression of the unique being that each of us is.

Today, the outer pressures are not as drastic as they have been in the past—the terribly recent past, in some cases— where failure to conform meant imprisonment or torture or even death. They are, however, more dangerous in a way because they are more insidious. These are the pressures to live like our neighbors, to think like our community, to re-shape ourselves in the image of someone else. The net result of this surrender is the destruction of the individual and the loss of his integrity. But the appeal is attractive, for it is the lure of the group, the promise of belonging.

It is a brave thing to have courage to be an individual; it is also, perhaps, a lonely thing. But it is better than not being an individual, which is to be nobody at all.

There are two very different kinds of conformity, but they tend, somewhere along the line, to blend, unless we are always aware of the difference. One of them is essential if human beings are to live with one another in a civilized way. That is social conformity, which is basically only a kind of good manners, which, in turn, is formalized kind-ness. The other, the dangerous one, is conformity to alien standards or ideas or values because that is the easy way, or because we think we can get farther in our job or profession by not fighting for what we believe in, or because we will be more popular if we surrender our own convictions to fit the community.

The trouble usually begins in childhood and it starts where most of our problems start, at home. Almost all children long to be popular, to be a part of their neighborhood group, to do exactly what all the other children do.

"Well, Susie can go to the movies during the week."

"You may go only on weekends," you say firmly.

"Why can't I?"

"Because it upsets our dinner hour, because I want you to study, because it is better for you not to keep late hours when you have to go to school the next day."

"Why do I have to be different?"

That, of course, is the key question in that first great battle—to conform or not to conform—which is heard in almost every family at some period or other.

Why do I have to be different? That is a question which has been effectively stilled in Russia, where one of the major objectives is to make sure that no one is different. There the research done by Pavlov in conditioning reflexes in dogs and other animals is, it seems to me, now used on men, wiping out their differences, "correcting" their individuality, which has no place in a Communist world; which is, indeed, inimical to it.

In the Soviet Union, according to a Rumanian psychologist, the Western type of mental therapy has been rejected. Instead, they have applied the Pavlovian system in an effort—a peaceful, nonviolent effort—to "recondition" men, to iron out their uniqueness, to mold them into tame, passive robots who will not only do as they are told without resistance but will *like* doing it.

This is assured by the Soviet training, which begins when the baby is two months old. At the age of fifty-seven days the baby goes into an institution, a nursery, while the mother returns to work. From the first day the child is trained to do his exercises, and all over Russia, in all the nurseries, the same thing is being done in exactly the same way.

The nurse takes the baby from its crib, lays it on the table and gives it a little massage and much the same kind of exercises we give our babies. If the baby cries, however, it is picked up at once and returned to its nice warm crib. Every day the same routine is observed until the baby begins to look forward to it. He enjoys the movements of his arms and legs, and stretching against a firm, friendly hand. He enjoys being twirled around on his head. There is no coercion, there is pleasure in all this.

As he grows older, he does more exercises, always with the same nurse, at the same hour, in the same place, in the same way. By the time he is a year and a half to two years old, he can go through a whole routine with other children. Not one word will be spoken until they have finally put on their shoes and marched out of the room just as they came in.

This is only the beginning of the kind of discipline needed to create the amenable, well-disciplined Communist citizen. There is no problem with the workers because the latter have been disciplined into conformity and will obey orders unquestioningly. Basically, they are as passively receptive to order as the baby is when he flexes his arms at the nurse's direction.

I myself in my work with the Soviets in the United Nations learned, by painful and exasperating experience, that they never give up a point. They are open neither to argument nor to reason. They are told what to say and they say it. They make a speech setting forth the position they have been ordered to take. You answer it carefully, point by point. All this is meticulously reported to Moscow. But unless instructions come to modify the point, the next day the Soviet delegate will get up and, ignoring entirely what has been said, repeat his original speech exactly as he had given it the day before.

The result of this ceaseless battle between individual and mass minds can be frustrating in the extreme. It can also be infuriating. But words, even when they seem to fail to communicate, are better than bombs. So we keep on trying. We must keep on trying. Sometimes we find that though we do not see eye to eye we can at least reach a *modus vivendi,* which is better than nothing.

There was a classic instance of this in the Human Rights Commission. One of the articles set forth the right to work. The representative of the Soviet Union said, "Our government is the only one which can give assurance of complying with this right. Our government controls every job and it will see that every citizen has a job because we need the work of every individual."

The United States representative replied, "We interpret this right to mean that a government has an obligation to create an economic climate in which every citizen who desires work can find the kind of work that he desires. In addition, the government has an obligation not to allow its citizens to starve. If, for reasons beyond their control, they are unable to find the kind of work they desire, the government is obliged to create work."

These two interpretations were read into the record at the time. Because there was no way for the two countries to agree, this article was accepted by each of us with our own interpretation.

Why do I have to be different? That is a question which I think every parent has an obligation to explain to his child. But he has no obligation to accept the child's idea that, because someone else does something, he must do it too. The sooner the child gets over thinking that he must do whatever everyone else does, the better for all concerned. It leads to living up to the Joneses, which is one of the real menaces of this country.

It horrifies me to realize how many people feel that it is incumbent on them to have something because their neighbors have it. They make their lives miserable until they get it, and often at the cost of some sacrifice. The worst of this is that, as frequently as not, they don't really want what the Joneses wanted; they are different people with different tastes and values.

Now and then, people tell me that there is a lot of good in this pressure to live up to the Joneses. It provides incentive, they say; it is a goad to ambition. But surely this is the wrong reason for ambition unless one wants to *be* Mr. Jones, which is ridiculous.

Your ambition should be to get as much life out of living as you possibly can, as much enjoyment, as much interest, as much experience, as much understanding. Not simply to be what is generally called "a success."

In a letter which came to me the other day I was asked if I would redefine the answer I once made to the question: "What do you consider success?"

The writer reminded me of the answer which I had given but wanted it restated and amplified because, he thought, many people today are groping for the real meaning of success.

I am inclined to think that being a success is tied up very closely with being one's own kind of individual.

At the time, I told the young man that there were, of course, many kinds of success. A vast majority of people seem to think that to be a financial success is all anyone has to be. And yet, it must be evident that such success, which boils down, after all, merely to being acquisitive on a large scale, cannot have value if it is bought at the expense of others. If you step on other people's necks to get rich, or barter your personal honor, then it is others who pay for your success and you can hardly call it your own.

If, however, you build something that is of benefit to other people, give them an opportunity to rise with you on your upward climb, you make a contribution.

Simply accumulating money is not, basically, a sign that one is a successful human being. A miser can do that, but as a man he is a failure. Success must include two things: the development of an individual to his utmost potentiality and a contribution of some kind to one's world.

Mozart, who was buried in a pauper's grave, was one of the greatest successes we know of, a man who in his early thirties had poured out his inexhaustible gift of music, leaving the world richer because he had passed that way. To leave the world richer—that is the ultimate success.

I believe firmly that the first indication on a child's part of a desire to have things because other people have them, and to do things because other people do them, should be corrected as quickly and as firmly as possible. It is a major and a far-reaching part of his education. It is his best refuge against the pressures he will undergo later on to surrender his individuality and to become a member of a faceless herd, too supine to take his courage in his hands and live his own life fully and completely.

I have made this point to many mothers who say, "Well, you simply can't do it. You can't convince a child that your way is better for him."

Of course you can't, unless you live up to your own beliefs. Children who have grown up in a home where people live according to their standards and expect them of their children will give little difficulty. The children will accept the standards their parents have set as examples. But, if it is all talk, if the parents say one thing and do another, the children will be antagonistic and will care nothing about what their parents want them to do.

For instance, if you tell a child that he can't have a bicycle just because the Jones boy has one, but at the same time you want a new washing machine like Mrs. Jones's and your husband is unhappy because Mr. Jones has a higher position than he, you have canceled your whole point.

But if you live what you believe, your children will believe it, too. I am thinking of a young family to whom the acquisition of a good record or a new book is a matter of rejoicing. Because the parents take such delight in these things and value them, the children have learned to handle the new book with care and to listen to the music with curiosity and interest, even when it is not rock 'n' roll. Once someone expressed surprise that one of the children recognized a Beethoven sonata.

"I ought to," he said. "We all listen to a new record as soon as it comes into the house, so I hear good music all the time."

These people aren't trying to "keep up" with anything but their own standards. They probably have the smallest and shabbiest car in their block, but it doesn't worry them. They are satisfied with the things they have because they get real enjoyment from them.

Children cannot just be told. They must see the values you preach put in practice if they are to become real.

I wish more people could believe this. Almost every day I see parents who insist on standards of conduct in their children which they make no pretense of following themselves. The child who is aware that his parents do not tell him the truth will assume that the practical method is to lie. The child who sees his parents sacrifice everything for material possessions will not believe that spiritual values are important. The child who is taught a kind of lip service to democracy but sees injustice or prejudice condoned by his parents will regard their preachments as empty and dishonest pretensions. If you want your child to develop as an honorable human being you have to practice what you preach.

One effective way of helping children to combat the pressures of conformity is to teach them to think for themselves. They should be trained to take part in home conversation, to form their own opinions, and then they should be encouraged to express these opinions. The trouble here, too often, is that the child must form many of his opinions from so little experience that he has insufficient data. But he should not have his opinion brushed aside with, "Oh, when you're older you'll make better sense," or "You don't know what you are talking about."

In my family there are vast differences of opinion on politics. All my sons love to argue and thrash out their ideas. I have always believed this is a healthy state of affairs unless they become too heated, at which time it is better to keep the argument amusing or, as a last resort, change the subject arbitrarily.

Of course, there is one problem involved in encouraging the young to express their opinions freely at home: that is, they can get into trouble outside the home if they take for granted that they will be listened to in the same way. They must learn to take into consideration the people they are with. This is what I mean by social conformity; not the sur-

render of one's beliefs but an awareness of when one is justified in forcing them and when it is not allowable if you have
good manners.

It should be a part of every young person's development
to learn to be aware of other people, to study them, not to
antagonize them if it can be avoided. It is all right to argue
to your heart's content at home, where divergences of opinion
are acceptable; but there are other homes and other groups
where older people are not willing to have a child express
his opinions, and the child must learn to feel his way. This
awareness of other people's desires and feelings is an important part of learning to live with other people and in a society.

I meet numbers of older people who do not want the
young to express an opinion. If the child is to be acceptable
as a guest he must learn when to keep quiet. Of course, I don't
mean that he should lie if he is directly asked, but he does not
have to push himself into expressing an opinion which may
be annoying to the people he is with.

It is important to keep before a child that he is not ex-
cused from having a conviction simply because he is in a
position where he should not express his opinion. In today's
life *you* must have convictions on basic questions. You must
make up your mind on where you stand. In the company of
your own peers you should be prepared to state where you
stand and defend your opinion. It is not enough to say, "I do
not agree at all." You must be able to say why.

I think it is essential that you should teach your child that
he has an intellectual and a spiritual obligation to decide for
himself what he thinks and not to allow himself to accept

what comes from others without putting it through his own reasoning process.

A child may sometimes worry you because he does not seem to fit into the group. Frequently, it would make life easier for him if he conformed. As Americans we simply must learn not to do this. Many people try to put everybody into a pattern; they think the same way and do the same things. But watch your child and you will learn that often what seems a mistake to you may be right for him.

Now and then, I hear complaints from my grandchildren because one does not want to do what the rest of the group does. I am interested since it is usually because one of them prefers to read rather than watch television, or, instead of swimming, wants to follow his own pet interest, something he does by himself. I have a grandnephew who is completely happy if he has a few spools, some wire, odds and ends of nails. He may be developing a communication system between a near-by house and our own. I do not know what he is doing and what value it may have. But I do know that it is wiser to let him develop his own interests, to respect his own individuality.

I do not mean for a moment that people should be aggressive about this business of living their lives according to their own lights. Much as I loathe and resist the idea of unreasoning conformity to any kind of pressure, I believe strongly in social conformity. This, as I have said, is largely a question of good manners. Too many people have forgotten good manners and their importance in smoothing and mak-

ing gracious and pleasant our dealing with our fellows. I am
not referring now to rigid rules of etiquette but to the simple
human kindness that is the foundation of all formal polite-
ness. Pulling out chairs for women, letting them pass through
a doorway first, rising for an older person. Just kindness. A
graciousness of manner which avoids hurting another person
or making him ill at ease. A graciousness of the heart.

But while this kind of conformity seems to me basic in
dealing with one's fellows, it does not imply that you alter
your own convictions and conform to theirs. As a rule, however, particularly if you find yourself in a neighborhood or a
profession or a job where your ideas are at a wide variance
from those of others, there is no necessity, no advantage, in
forcing your ideas down their throats. If you live steadfastly
in accordance with them, you will eventually gain respect for
your stand.

This is your life, not someone else's. It is your own feeling of what is important, not what people will say. Sooner
or later, you are bound to discover that you cannot please
all of the people around you all of the time. Some of them
will attribute to you motives you never dreamed of. Some of
them will misinterpret your words and actions, making them
completely alien to you. So you had better learn fairly early
that you must not expect to have everyone understand what
you say and what you do.

The important thing is to be sure that those who love
you, whether family or friends, understand as nearly as you
can make them understand. If they believe in you, they will
trust your motives. But do not ask or expect to have anyone

with you on everything. Do not try for it. To reach such a state of unanimity would mean that you would risk losing your own individuality to attain it.

I never can understand why so many people are afraid to live their own lives as they themselves think is right. You can get rid of your neighbors but you cannot get rid of yourself, so you are the person to be satisfied.

I am always delighted when I see people who express their own personalities in the way that is right for them. In clothes, for instance. Most people anxiously follow current styles, whether or not they suit the individual or his needs. Personally, I like simple clothes and comfort. I do not concern myself much with fashion. I choose my clothes with an eye to what will make me most comfortable and fit my particular needs.

I like to remember an elderly friend of mine and of my grandmother to whom I used to take my children when they were small. In a standardized world she kept her own individuality, her own atmosphere, an oasis of peace and quiet in a world grown increasingly shrill. I can see her now, presiding with gentle dignity over her great silver tea tray, a dainty Dresden china figure, white hair piled high, wearing always either a white or a lilac gown with a train. Her clothes were right for her and she never changed with current fashions.

Wanda Landowska, the great harpsichordist, who recently died in her eighties, maintained, with gentle persistence, her own integrity as a personality as well as a musician. She had found a mode of dress that suited her, long flowing dresses and velvet ballet slippers. Whether at home

or on the concert stage she stuck to her chosen form of dressing. She didn't look odd. She looked like Landowska. How
many of us, I wonder, dare to look like ourselves?

This same tendency to conformity exists more and more
in the one place which should most definitely be our own—
our home. The house should be the product of your own
personality. The furniture should suit your way of life, the
pictures be pictures you love, the colors be the ones you enjoy.
If you call in a decorator and say, "Please do this room," without expressing any likes or dislikes of your own, you have abdicated any expression of your personality.

Of course, if you have seen something you deliberately
want to copy, a room or some piece of furniture that you
respond to and particularly like, you will still be making a
background that reflects your own interests and taste and
personality. It is when you surrender your own tastes to an
impersonal background that you are apt to end, rootless, in
meaningless surroundings.

When my husband and I were on our wedding trip we
saw in a French château some cane furniture with brown
carved wood, stiff chairs, and a sofa, and we ordered some
like them to use in a drawing room at home. We would never
have given someone a blanket order to furnish a French room
if we had not been charmed and wanted to have something to
re-create for us an experience we cared to remember.

Of course, this means you must have a certain confidence in your own taste. And here, I think, is the key to much
conformity—the lack of self-confidence that makes people
fearful of following their own bent. And here, too, much can

be done by parents at home to provide the kind of education that will give you assurance that you can trust your own taste. Without seeing beautiful things, without being familiar with how a color can be made to give charm to a room, you will be afraid of what you put into a room and how it will look.

My secretary, Miss Thompson, was with me for thirty years. At one time I was furnishing her apartment. She could not decide on what she wanted for curtains and rugs. At length, I went with her to look at material.

"I looked for a month," Tommy said. "You decided at once."

"That was partly because you were afraid of spending my money," I told her. "But in the second place you were afraid to decide because you did not know whether you would like your choice. I was willing to take a chance."

Little by little, as she traveled with me in Europe and at home, and saw beautiful things, she began to be more discriminating and to know what she liked. In time, she was sure of her own taste and had the courage to back it.

Remember always that you have not only the right to be an individual; you have an obligation to be one. *You cannot make any useful contribution in life unless you do this.*

There is a growing tendency in large organizations to require a great deal of conformity among their employees, especially conformity in thinking, though a certain amount of conformity in behavior and even in dress is being stressed. This is occasionally referred to as "dynamic conformity," an amusingly paradoxical term that seems to be an attempt to sugar-coat the pill. It strikes me as curious that the large organizations, which are almost always conservative in their views, come closer to attempting to create the Soviet Pavlovian man than any other group.

This whole tendency is singularly shortsighted. When a man has lost—or deliberately abdicated—his own individuality, his contribution is to a great extent diminished. He has less originality to bring to his job, less value in every way. Unless he can maintain his own unique quality, the sharp cutting edge of his personal views, he is simply reflecting other men's views and is therefore comparatively valueless.

It was the flexibility, the originality, and the independence of thought—combined, of course, with our vast resources—that made American business grow so rapidly. If the seeds of growth are made sterile, if men become passive followers instead of developing qualities of leadership— and courage—we may find someday that our way of life has been superseded.

Many people tell me bitterly that today they cannot "afford" to keep their individuality, that if they want to "get ahead" they must conform. My answer is that no one can afford not to be a man. No position can compensate for coming face to face with a robot when you are alone. And I remember, too, a man who asked, "Get ahead of whom? There is no one I want to shove past. I just want to get ahead of myself, make myself as big as I can, but not measure myself by someone else."

I have often heard that in order to keep a job you will have to make compromises. But make them as little as you can, and in your private life try to live in the way you really feel you want to live. It will change even the business conditions under which you may have to struggle.

The trouble is that not enough people have come together with the firm determination to live the things which they say they believe. Spinoza once made a profound comment: "Men believe a thing when they behave as though it were true."

Perhaps you have to make the compromise, but I wonder if you do not pay too high a price for it, if it does not have a detrimental effect on character. You have to learn to live with yourself. Are you going to feel you have weakened yourself as a person because you didn't stand for something you thought was fundamentally right?

People have to weigh their compromises. There is no question, I suppose, that you will have to make them. But if you are sure that you are not losing sight of your objective, that you have moved forward even a little bit, you can justify your compromise within the general framework. Often people are not ready to move with you the whole way and you must go a step at a time. As long as you have taken a single step you have not abandoned your objective. But if you give up, you have done something you cannot justify to yourself. That is what hurts you. You know you did not have the courage.

With the development of automation a greater number of people will find that the right to be an individual is more and more difficult to exercise. We can lose individuality and decrease the opportunities to develop personality. And yet this is most important in a country where we pride ourselves that the individual is a vital unit in our civilization.

The constant pressure to bring about conformity is a dangerous thing. People are so bombarded with certain sayings, told so often what they should believe, that sometimes they don't know what to believe. But they must find out where they stand, make up their own minds what they really think. That is why I am convinced that every effort must be made in childhood to teach the young to use their own minds. For one thing is sure: If they don't make up their minds, someone will do it for them.

People often write, taking me to account for the fact that my children have made mistakes in marriage and been divorced. I can only answer that one has no right, once one's children are grown and mature, to interfere with their decisions. If asked, you should state how you feel, how you think. But until asked, it is an intrusion to thrust your ideas on any grown human being. And if, when you do express yourself, there is a difference between you, you must respect the inherent thing with which you have endowed the child: the right of decision.

Someone once asked my husband why he did not tell a certain child not to get a divorce when he was running for the Presidency.

"What my children do about their lives," he answered, "is their own concern. It has nothing to do with whether or not my policies are accepted by the people. I do not expect the people will hold me responsible for what my children do. I must stand on my own feet and answer for my own judgment and what I do myself."

chapter 8

How to Get the Best Out of People

Nobody really does anything alone. For almost every achievement in life, it is essential to deal with other people. Even great leaders, like Lincoln, Gandhi and Churchill, were able to establish leadership alone, but they had to have a following in order to bring about the desired results. It is only by inducing others to go along that changes are accomplished and work is done.

One of the essential points we must bring home to our children is that there is comparatively little they can do entirely by themselves. So, along with the need for individual development, there is also an equally pressing need to work co-operatively. This, of course, involves learning about people and finding out how to draw the best from your association with them.

Mutual respect is the basis of all civilized human relationships. It is necessary in the family group, it is inseparable from friendship, it is a requirement in the work one does with one's associates on whatever level, and it is increasingly necessary in seeking co-operation among the peoples of the world.

There is a terrible, a poignant, need among people in a world of increasing automation to be recognized as individuals who stand out from the crowd for a moment, and not simply to be members of a faceless group. I still remember the painful feeling I had when a man employed for many years by a large organization remarked proudly, "The elevator man knows me. I don't have to tell him at what floor to stop for me."

That need for a sense of individuality is in every human being and one must not ignore it. Without recognition one has a rootless feeling. It is like the legendary Antaeus. While he could touch the earth he was invulnerable. When he was lifted, he was easily conquered.

There is a great deal in learning the techniques of handling people and the earlier one learns it the better off he will be and the smoother his life will become. Next to that foundation of respect for others, which should be instilled in every child, one should form the habit of really *seeing* the people one meets, paying attention to them so that one will be able to recognize them the next time and give them a sense of individuality.

When the present Queen Mother of England, then the young Queen Elizabeth, accompanied the King on his visit to the United States, she made an enormous number of friends by a simple action. As she drove or walked through great

throngs of people she would pick out individuals in the crowd
and really look at them. After she had passed, people would
say with delight, "The Queen looked at me!"

This was something that had never occurred to me as
being possible on a mass basis and I found it an excellent lesson. Instead of trying to look at all the people, which is impossible, I would single out a child or one or two individuals,
Everyone in the vicinity of that person would feel that I had
singled him out and had paid personal attention to him.

This, though I have illustrated it on a mass scale, is what
should be done in dealing with individuals. I confess that for
a long time, at tea parties at the White House, I really did not
identify many of the people who streamed past me. At first,
this was partly fatigue until I grew accustomed to standing and shaking hands. But partly it was because I felt that
merely seeing people move past did not mean anything any-
way. Not until much later did I discover that if you really look
at people and shake hands warmly as if you mean it and are
not performing a mechanical gesture, you give them a feeling
of closeness.

I will have to admit that at times the result is a little awkward. Years after one of these fleeting meetings I have had
people say, "I shook hands with you in the White House."
Obviously, they expect me to remember. Sometimes this is a
trifle bewildering, but it has real value for the individual and
does give a sense of recognition if, even for a moment, you
concentrate on the person who is before you.

During my trip to the South Pacific during the Second
World War, I walked through miles and miles of hospital

wards, greeting as many of the wounded men as I humanly
could. Today, so many years later, I constantly meet men, in
almost every state and often abroad, who say, "Oh, you remember me! I was in the fourth bed in the second row on the
left. We talked about my home town . . . my family . . . my
civilian job."

Shamelessly, for I cannot bear to admit their faces have
blurred into a kaleidoscopic picture of wounded men, I say,
"Of course, I remember." And sometimes, prompted by some
particular incident that happened at the time, I really do.
But though, too often, I have forgotten, at least the memory of
a friendly hand, a link with their distant home, a heartening
message from their Commander in Chief, had remained as a
token of a fleeting moment.

If you approach each new person you meet in a spirit of adventure you will find that you become increasingly interested in them and endlessly fascinated by the new channels
of thought and experience and personality that you encounter. I do not mean simply the famous people of the world, but
people from every walk and condition of life. You will find
them a source of inexhaustible surprise because of the unexpected qualities and interests which you will unearth in your
search for treasure. But the treasure is there if you will mine
for it.

If such a search is to be successful, however, you will
need two qualities which you can develop by practice. One is
the ability to be a good listener. The other is the imaginative
ability to put yourself in the other person's place; to try to

discover what he is thinking and feeling; to understand as far as you can the background from which he came, the soil out of which his roots have grown, the customs and beliefs and ideas which have shaped his thinking.

While, of course, it is much easier for an older person of experience to do this, it is essential to begin young, in order to store up the experiences, which will increase and become usable with maturity. You can establish an understanding relationship with people who are entirely outside your own orbit if you care enough to make the effort, to see the people you are looking at, to understand them.

It was by sitting and talking with miners' wives that I came really to know what they thought and felt, what it was like to be a miner's wife. This awareness did not come at once. It never does. But countless times during the years of the great depression I sat in their small kitchens, sometimes with their husbands, sometimes without them, but always with a group of children too young to go to school hanging around their mother's skirts. Often a sick child lay on the only bed and when I asked where the others slept the mother would point out a little closet with no outside windows and with sacking on the floor as the only bedding.

Listening to such a woman talk, taking in the surroundings, one finds oneself, little by little, coming to understand the feelings of that other human being. Intellectually, one may have known for years that certain needs exist, but until one sees with one's own eyes and comes to feel with one's own heart, one will never understand other people.

*   *   *

If you are to get along with people, if you are to get the best out of your dealings with them, on whatever level, it is not enough merely to win their confidence. You must be able to estimate the extent to which you succeed in communicating with them. With no grasp of their background or point of view, you are apt to find yourself talking in a vacuum. You aren't reaching people.

To be able to reach people! That is a quality which actors acquire because they must learn to gauge their audience. Helen Gahagan Douglas said that her training as an actress had been of great value in her political career. She had learned to watch her audience for its reactions. When she became aware that she wasn't putting across what she meant or making the impression she intended, she would change her speech, if necessary, and couch it in terms that would be more effective.

I used to think that the reason my husband's fireside chats were so successful was largely that he had learned to state complicated questions in a clear and simple way so that no one could fail to understand him. Often he would illustrate his point by citing conversations he had had during his brief visits to Hyde Park with his farmer neighbors. These were human incidents on a local scale, but he used them frequently to clarify complicated questions of government.

I know a young man who became extremely successful in speaking to students. He never failed to establish an immediate communication because he understood their point of view and tried to put himself in their place. This, perhaps, is the chief secret of getting along with people. At one time this young man was head of the National Student Organization; since then he has filled many different positions.

Listening while he addressed student groups, I learned from him how much it means to remember how you felt yourself when you were in another person's position. For instance, he knew how a young man would feel when he was drafted into one of the armed services and went through basic training. He remembered how senseless some of the rules and regulations seemed until the draftee had enough experience to understand their purpose. Some of these rules, he admitted to his audience, still did not make much sense to him.

He used this point as a start in discussing government problems and he reached and held the attention of people who had given little thought to such problems. But he invariably put across what he had to say, identified himself with his audience, discussed the young men who would go out of school or college to the impersonal machine of the armed services; from that he led them easily to a discussion of what was required for defense, what its needs were for the protection of the country, what its demands must be on an individual. But he established it as an individual problem; he reached the heart of his audience before he attempted to launch into his main theme.

There are always a few people, sometimes unfortunately in important positions, who feel that they can deal with others only by imposing their will, by giving orders, by taking a dictatorial—master to serf—attitude. Sometimes, of course, it works. The orders are obeyed. But they are often obeyed at the price of resentment and the loss of self-respect. Obedience may have its uses, but it is no substitute for willing, unco-erced co-operation.

I suppose one of the commonest complaints people have to make in regard to their dealings with others is about the dreadful time they have in coping with their employees, whether in their homes or on the job. I always want to ask these dissatisfied people what kind of time the employees have with them, whether they are treated with respect and consideration, whether their employer recognizes them as individuals, whether he gives them the assurance that he be-lieves in them, whether he gives them praise when it is earned and a just measure of acknowledgment. Surely this is a small thing compared with the results it brings in stimulus and in-creased effort. And yet, no matter how avid they themselves may be for praise and appreciation, people are often niggardly in giving it to others, however merited it is.

Over the years, I have had occasion to work with many committees, almost countless committees, it seems at times. It is a source of endless interest to watch the ways in which the chairmen of these committees have succeeded or bungled fatally in handling the people with whom it was their pur-pose to work co-operatively for a common goal. How often I have seen the task bog down in unnecessary failure simply because a man could not handle the people who were associ-ated with him.

Sometimes this was a result of self-satisfaction, of the man's feeling that he had nothing to learn from his colleagues. I don't know of an attitude that succeeds more quickly in

antagonizing people. I know, for instance, of the chairman
of a school board who was too arrogant to explain what he
wanted and why he wanted it. His objectives were excellent,
but because of his attitude he failed to carry anyone with him
and the schools in his community are now practically without funds and the children have neither school lunches nor
buses. That is a heavy price to pay for arrogance.

I have never known anyone to succeed over a period of
time in dealing with people, particularly in committee work,
if he assumed an air of complete self-sufficiency and behaved
as though he had no need for the support or assistance of his
colleagues. Yet it must be obvious that one of the most effective techniques in dealing with people is to appeal to them
for their help. If they think you are in need of their assistance and that you will appreciate it, they are apt to do their
best to help fill your need.

Naturally, in working with a group of people you must
keep constantly in mind that you are dealing with a variety
of human individuals. Some will want to be recognized as
superior intelligences. Others will hope to remain in absolute
anonymity. To weld any group together and get them to do
the maximum possible work, in one way or another, is not an
easy thing. The key problem is to find some binding interest
to make them feel a part of the whole, and to stimulate each
one to make his own particular contribution.

Of course, you are not going to establish this diversity-
through-unity unless you have first given them all a clear
picture of the objective, of the needs that must be met. But if
you can do this, and if you can *listen*, you will find that each

one will volunteer gladly to make his particular contribution.

You can, as I have learned by long experience, with intelligence and many trial efforts, learn to work in and with a group, learn to understand people who are completely different from anyone you have ever encountered before. But it takes patience, being willing to listen, and trying to understand how they think and feel.

It requires, too, a greater emphasis on the main goal than on one's own vanity. As an example, in group work I have often seen a person make what was actually a sound suggestion. Someone, however, challenges the idea. At once the person who put it forward storms and protests, is indignant that his idea was not accepted, and as a result he gets nowhere at all. The idea is firmly rejected.

But suppose he had accepted the criticisms without challenging them. Suppose someone came up with another idea. Our protagonist's objective is, or should be, to see that the best idea is agreed upon. Instead of resisting the criticism with anger, he will, if he is wise, accept it with humility. He will consider the other person's idea and, if he can, he will go along with it, making tentative suggestions for improvements until it is gradually modified and comes much closer to his main objective.

Eventually, it is quite possible that a third person, perhaps one who was antagonistic to his original idea, will come up triumphantly with a suggestion which, incorporating the tentative changes, is practically the same as his own. Now if the protagonist is thinking primarily about the objective, he will be delighted. But if he is interested primarily in getting

YOU LEARN BY LIVING

personal credit for the achievement, he is quite likely to lose everything. In group work, it is certainly the better part of wisdom to take the result and let the credit go.

In the long run, whether in community affairs, in business, or in government, it is the individual who can assimilate and then throw out ideas who will make a broader and more valuable contribution than the one who forgets that he is not dealing primarily with ideas: he is dealing with people through whom those ideas have to filter.

If it is essential, though difficult, to learn how to deal with various kinds of people in one's own environment, it is equally essential, and much more difficult, to learn how to deal with various kinds of people from a totally different environment, people of many races and cultures, people whose customs and patterns of thought are altogether unlike our own. At this moment, it is quite possible that the future of the world and of life on this planet depends on our ability to master the technique of getting along with the many different peoples who inhabit this globe.

One of the major elements is to be willing to learn about the customs and modes of thought and background of the peoples of many lands with whom we must, now and henceforth, establish a new mode of life. Too many of us feel that any custom which is not our own is ridiculous or essentially wrong, that it is fair game for laughter or contempt. We could make no more devastating or stupid—yes, stupid—mistake. To show a lack of respect for another person's customs is fatal to any enduring or self-respecting relationship.

One can, of course, quite unintentionally blunder and of-
fend because of a lack of knowledge of the customs of another
country. I remember some young people telling me of a meeting where a number of different nationalities were brought
together. The chairman was a young man of little experience
in such work. He had no knowledge of how the customs of
other countries differed from his own and he still had not
learned how essential it is to acquire such information before
one can deal effectively with foreigners.

With great enthusiasm he described some activities
which he planned for group action, in which both the young
men and the young women would join. To his shocked surprise he nearly broke up the meeting. At that time, equality
among young men and women in Japan was unheard of, un-
seemly and improper.

Only when he understood the situation could the
young man offer a different approach to the problem, which
achieved his objective without doing violence to the customs
of either side. This seems to me to be the ideal solution. As
a people, I am afraid, we tend too often to brush aside with
impatience, sometimes with discourtesy, customs and points
of view which are alien to us. If the way is not our way it is
wrong!

Here, perhaps, lies the key to our growing failure to win
friends abroad, though we have, in every other respect, richly
earned that friendship, in money, material support, and
human kindness that asks no return. We have failed only in
enlightened understanding and tolerance—and respect.

It is not our job to change other people's customs. It is

our job to know what they are and, if possible, to understand them. Not that this is always easy. For instance, what young woman in this country could understand the Japanese custom of the pouch?

I learned of this through a young Japanese newspaper woman, who told me, "Our great trouble, Mrs. Roosevelt, is the system of the pouch."

I looked at her without understanding.

"Oh, aren't you familiar with it? In every Japanese family, the oldest woman, who is head of the women of the household, has a leather pouch into which every member of the family is expected to put his earnings. She doles out to each one what she thinks he or she needs. With our changing way of life, this is becoming difficult for us, and the young women are beginning to rebel."

When I first went to India I liked very much the Indian custom of greeting people by putting your hands together instead of shaking hands. One day, at a big reception in Bombay I watched the host moving from table to table where the guests were seated, eating. As the women came in they would greet each table with this pretty gesture.

At length, I was asked to go on the balcony to greet a tremendous crowd. What was I going to do? I could not wave, as one does in the United States, so I decided to try their greeting. Because I was willing to make that little outward gesture which was theirs I received a terrific ovation. Surely it is a small thing to do, to acknowledge and respect the customs and habits of another. And it brings with it a rich harvest of mutual esteem and liking.

When I was in Thailand I learned that a Buddhist priest, who wears a yellow robe, cannot shake hands; he must never touch a woman. Stupidly, I forgot this custom. When I was at Yale, talking to the foreign students, I saw a young Buddhist priest, an exchange student, standing in the director's office. Impulsively I extended my hand. In the flash of a moment I knew that I had blundered.

"Please," I said to the director, "say I knew his customs but that I forgot temporarily; I meant no disrespect and I greet him warmly."

Even people who go abroad for business firms or the government sometimes have not been thoroughly enough briefed on the customs of the country they are visiting. If they are sensitive, this awareness of their own ignorance, their unpreparedness, makes them nervous about attempting to acquire new friends. As a result, they restrict themselves to the colony of their own compatriots, or, at most, a few others whose language and customs they understand. Obviously, this cuts down tremendously on the value of our contacts with the peoples of the world. We simply haven't bothered to know them well. This is a mistake which the Soviets do not make. Before going out of their own country, they are not only thoroughly familiar with the language of the land to which they are sent, but they are thoroughly briefed on its customs.

Not long ago, a wise statesman from another country said to me, "The United States has given more in money and goods to help the peoples of the world than almost any other country, and yet you receive less real gratitude and have, I think, made fewer real friends."

I asked, of course, whether this was because nobody ever likes to be on the receiving end only, and because we have not shown a willingness to receive as well as give.

The answer was that while this might enter into it, he thought on the whole it came from the fact that most of us, in meeting the peoples of the world, do not give them a feeling of warmth, of a real desire to know these new people we are coming in contact with. And, by staying apart, we give no feeling that we share their experiences, which might make our lavish giving more acceptable.

I cannot overemphasize how essential it is that we show respect for the customs of people from foreign countries, and particularly people from different cultures and environments. Whenever possible, I feel that, in dealing with them, we should try as far as is practicable to accept their ways. I remember how excited the Japanese were, trying to teach me the use of chopsticks. I never did it well, but at least I was willing to try.

On the other hand, there are times when one may really disapprove of a foreign custom, when one cannot condone it. In such cases, one can show one's disapproval without words or the slightest antagonism. For instance, it is the habit in Japan for a woman to walk behind her husband. I certainly did not think any woman should be put in this position. So when I was walking with a man and his wife, I managed always to keep him abreast of us and not permit him to get ahead. In this way, without any comment or criticism, I made it clear that this was a custom which, to the Westerner, seemed to indicate a disrespect for women which we could not condone or accept.

There was a time, a generation ago, when the average person in this country was apt to meet comparatively few strangers from other lands. Of course, there was a great influx of immigrants, but these, in the overwhelming majority, were eager to absorb our ways and blend into our environment as quickly as possible. Today, the whole picture has changed. Though our immigration laws have greatly restricted the number of people coming to take on citizenship, we have more and more people from every corner of the world coming here on foreign missions, in association with the United Nations, in all sorts of groups and for many purposes, people who are maintaining their distinctive dress and customs and modes of thought.

We talk so often about the differences between people, yet here in our country we find that, in spite of circumstances which create great differences, we have certain great similarities. Rich or poor, we want our children to be well educated. Rich or poor, we want them to do better than we have done. Rich or poor, we want the respect of our neighbors and perhaps their affection. Love and death come to us all, no matter what the circumstances of our lives. In the big things that matter, the similarities are far greater than the differences.

If this is true at home it is true anywhere in the world. People want the same things. They strive for the same things. They suffer from the same things. The differences are important but often superficial. The basic things are similar.

No one, I think, can deny that for the welfare of all of us we must learn to deal with foreign peoples, not simply in our own way, but with mutual respect and understanding and acceptance of their ways. I am convinced that it is as important for any young person to learn to respect the individuality of others as it is for him to respect his own. For, as I said in the beginning, nobody really does anything alone. We need all the friendship, all the support, we can get. But they have to be earned.

chapter 9

Facing Responsibility

We all create the person we become by our choices as we go through life. In a very real sense, by the time we are adult, *we are the sum total of the choices we have made*.

This is not pleasant hearing for the person who wishes to place the responsibility for what he has become on someone else or on that blanket alibi, circumstances beyond his control. To such a person the circumstances always seem to be beyond his control. But I believe most firmly that in the long run every single one of us must be responsible for himself and for his actions.

I am sometimes taken to task for my point of view, for laying so much stress on the fact that we are responsible for ourselves; that, in the long run, everyone must achieve this responsibility by himself and for himself. Remember, people tell me, the tremendous assistance that is available today through psychiatry and psychoanalysis. Of course, I am aware that a great deal of help is possible and I am grateful for the fact that it exists, often preventing frustration and despair which, in the past, led to tragic situations.

But I think, too, that there is a possible danger here. In the very desire for help one is apt to forget that the objective should be to enable the individual to stand on his own feet. Sometimes people cling to this outside assistance, reluctant to let go of the support and stand alone.

The kind of self-reliance I have in mind goes farther than mere responsibility for oneself. Each of us, ultimately, is responsible in large part for the welfare of his community, for the kind of government he has, for the world he lives in.

This is not an easy situation. It is particularly difficult today when so many of our familiar landmarks have gone, socially, economically, politically, internationally. There was a spiritual safety in what was old and established and familiar; in what was, or seemed to be, permanent. People knew what was expected of them. They understood the conditions they had to deal with. They accepted the dogmas of their period.

But today where are these familiar things? Where are these known conditions? Where is the old safety? Instead, we find ourselves in an unfamiliar world, attempting to deal with unknown factors, having to blaze new trails for ourselves.

"Anxiety," Kierkegaard said, "is the dizziness of freedom." This freedom of which men speak, for which they fight, seems to some people a perilous thing. It has to be earned at a bitter cost and then—it has to be lived with. For freedom makes a huge requirement of every human being. With freedom comes responsibility. For the person who is unwilling to grow up, the person who does not want to carry his own weight, this is a frightening prospect.

We must all face an unpalatable fact that we have, too often, a tendency to skim over; we proceed on the assumption that all men want freedom. This is not as true as we would like it to be. There are many men and women who are far happier when they have relinquished their freedom, when someone else guides them, makes their decisions for them, takes the responsibility for them and for their actions. They don't want to make up their minds. They don't want to stand on their own feet.

I have often thought that so much attention is paid to the aggressive sins, such as violence and cruelty and greed with all their tragic effects, that too little attention is paid to the passive sins, such as apathy and laziness, which in the long run can have a more devastating and destructive effect upon society than the others.

It is self-evident that one of the first things which our children must learn is to face full responsibility for their actions, to make their own choices and cope with the results. Not only their stature as adult human beings requires this, but the whole democratic system which is now at stake depends upon it. For our system is founded on self-government, which is untenable if the individuals who make up the system are unable to govern themselves.

It is, I think, true that almost all children are convinced, at some time in their young lives, that their upbringing and home training are a source of unhappiness, and that their environment is responsible for what they may do with their lives later on. No one can face the fact of his own responsibility for a drastic mistake or for weakness in his own character without some degree of pain. It is easier to place this burden on someone else or on circumstances.

"It wasn't my fault." That is an almost instinctive reaction to failure of any kind. But this is the point of cleavage between the mature and the immature individual. The mature person will admit, "It was my fault. The mistake was of my own making. Now that I understand why it happened, why I made the wrong choice, I'll try not to make the same mistake again."

But the person who clings to his alibi, "It wasn't my fault," not only is lying to himself but he is evading his responsibility. He will make the same mistake over and over and continue to feel terribly sorry for himself. The circumstances were beyond his control, weren't they?

Why should we shy away with shame from having made a mistake? No human being is all-wise; no human being always lives up to the best that he is capable of. Failure comes to everyone, except when one does nothing at all, which in itself is a failure. All we can do is to be honest with ourselves, be humble and try, as we gain wisdom, to rectify our mistakes and possibly to avoid some of them.

There is a time, in childhood, when it seems possible that there is a clear, a final answer to everything "in the back of the book," where the correct solutions to the arithmetic problems are to be found—or used to be. But with the familiar landmarks gone, there are fewer and fewer final answers. Even the questions are new. The responsibility has come to each of us to work out for ourselves what we believe to be right or wrong. We have to learn to think things through for ourselves.

Nearly every one of us, at some time or other, thinks what a great waste and pity it is that the older generation cannot teach the younger generation, cannot share their experiences, cannot save the young their mistakes; that each human being has to learn by his own experience and his own mistakes. And yet it is possible that this is the best way. After all, so much that the older generation learned is wrong! And perhaps they didn't always learn as much by their experience as they thought they did.

Certainly, it requires considerable humility to answer children's questions, to guide them in their thinking and behavior. One would have to be sure of his infallibility to lay down absolute rules of right and wrong, good and bad.

My mother-in-law often used to say to me, "Why don't you tell the children not to do this or to do that?"

"Because," I would reply, "I'm not sure that my way is best for them."

"Of course you are sure, my dear," she would say firmly. "There is only one right and one wrong."

She saw everything in black and white; there were no grays. Certain things were wrong, others were right, without any shading. And she could not take in the fact that many of her rules were based on conventions, on social conditions, on a whole frame of reference that had ceased to exist by the time she had become a grandmother.

There are, of course, a number of older people who stick firmly to the old ways, without any interest in what has happened to the world. "I was always brought up to think. . . ." they begin, and you know at once that they will bring forth a rule of behavior or a point of view that has no particular relevance now.

Often we demand of youth an ability to think through and make up their minds at too early an age, when they would rather have definite rules laid down for them. But, as they will have to learn in modern society to think things through and make their own choices for themselves, the sooner we can help them to do this the better.

The first time the child is required to make his or her own decision or choice he may, simply because the situation is novel, be dismayed. For instance, the first time a little girl asks, "What dress shall I wear to school?" and her mother, knowing they are equally appropriate, says, "You must decide that," the child may be reluctant to do so. She is not sure her choice is right; she doesn't want the responsibility; she is also a little afraid that some necessary support has been withdrawn from her.

The first time Johnny breaks a window when he is playing ball and is told that he is responsible, that he must go to the homeowner and take the blame, he will probably be not only shocked but indignant. He feels that a parent should be a bulwark and a shelter against trouble. Of course, if the child is made to feel too guilty he will be apt to try to cover up the next peccadillo. But if you explain the situation, appeal to his manhood rather than his babyhood, you are more than likely to get co-operation, and willing co-operation.

It is wise to observe children while they are growing, to watch their actions and reactions, so that you can become aware of the first indications of a desire to shirk responsibility. Often you hear mothers say, "If I leave it to Tom I know it will be done, but you just can't depend on Dick. He's apt to go off and play tennis and forget all about it."

At this point, Dick must be taught that he cannot shirk his responsibility. Sometimes, perhaps, it is better to enforce a penalty: no tennis until he has fulfilled his obligations. For shirking is insidious because it is so easy. If it is condoned, it may well become a habit.

There is no human growth without the acceptance of responsibility and I think it should be developed as soon as it reasonably can be. In too many families there seems to be one person who shoulders the responsibility for all, copes with the problems, makes the decisions, does the chores, looks after the sick or the elderly.

In the family, responsibility should, if at all possible, be a community concern, in which all share to the extent of their capacities. This joint responsibility is easy for the young, and, having experienced it early, it is much easier to assume responsibility later on, taking for granted that this is the only possible course of action. The child who grows up with the "Let George do it" point of view will probably shelve responsibility all his life.

Curiously enough, it is often the people who refuse to assume any responsibility who are apt to be the sharpest critics
of those who do.

How is the money to be spent? This is one of the most vital
problems to be solved in any family and it is one of the most
far-reaching. It determines where your basic values lie: What
do you want in exchange for the money you earn? The answer
to this problem must be a matter of joint responsibility.

Incomes vary tremendously in this country, and in many
others, ranging from vast wealth to what is barely subsistence. It is pointless to discuss what is "enough" money. No
two people would be likely to agree on what is "enough."
Even people of exactly the same wage-earning group would
disagree violently as to whether they had enough.

Aside from basic subsistence, a shelter, clothing, sufficient food, few people want the same things out of life or
out of their money. Some people don't actually know what
they want. They are straining every nerve to have what their
neighbors have, as though their prestige and their happiness,
which they often count as one and the same, depended on
keeping up with artificial standards.

Planning the budget and allotting the income should, I
think, be a unifying force in the family, a matter for group
discussion and decision. Children should understand what
the family situation is, how much money there is to be allotted for different things, so that they will not make unreasonable demands, and they will have a feeling of responsibility,
even when they are not actually earning part of the income.

Financial planning should be a part of family life and it should start from the very beginning. For the bulk of the people of this country all the income is derived from the salaries of one or at most two members of the family. The first step in that financial planning is to make a clear and honest evaluation of what you want to have, not just in things, but in the way of living itself. You've got to clarify your own values, to see what is most important to you. The tragedy of too much financial planning in this country is that much of it is based on false values, on a striving and sacrificing for things that have no commensurate value for the person who buys them.

Beyond the point of meeting basic needs—food, shelter, clothing, medical protection, education, recreation—one comes face to face with what one wants not simply out of money but out of life. For my own part, what I want out of money is chiefly a sense of achievement. To live upon an income for which I had not worked would make me uneasy. I like to feel I can pit my ability to earn against others, that there is something I can do to earn that money. In itself the money, as mere accumulation, does not, I really believe, have value for many Americans. What has value is what can be accomplished by the money, is the widened scope of activities and interests it can provide, is the pleasure it can give to others.

I have not touched on the point that every member of the family should have some small sum of his own to spend, in order to teach him how to handle money and how to make choices. In some cases, even the youngest child in the family is expected to earn this, whether just as spending money or whether he is expected to be responsible for buying his own clothes.

I have a little grandnephew who has been put on an allowance out of which he is expected to buy his own clothes. Lately I have been observing with some amusement that his wardrobe is growing scantier and scantier because he always needs some new scientific equipment. I remember when my husband always had money to buy a new and fascinating first edition of a book, but he would frequently answer a protest of mine by saying he could not possibly afford to buy any new shirts.

I know a family which has its own highly individual method of tackling group problems. When the father appears at the breakfast table on Sunday mornings wearing a large cowboy hat, everyone knows there are problems to be discussed. After breakfast, they all gather in the living room, each wearing a special hat, ranging from a high silk hat to a clown's peaked cap or a chef's white hat. Father, mother, and children, down to the youngest boy, gather together, wearing their absurd hats, and thrash out the immediate problem.

It may be that there has been an illness with an unexpected drain on the income and therefore curtailments will have to be made in the budget. Everyone suggests ways of doing this, each volunteers the thing he is willing to do without. It may be the question of taking a motherless boy into the home for a couple of years and helping him with his education, a situation which would mean the three sons would have to do without certain things. It may be a question of choice: we can afford either a good record player or a television set. Which is it to be?

Because of the absurd picture they make, wearing their ridiculous hats in the midst of all this serious discussion, they never get overheated and angry in the course of the debates that follow. But they have accomplished more than words could express in knitting a family together and making the solving of budget problems a matter of shared responsibility.

Certainly, there can be no question that open discussion of problems can bring with it a sense of mutual confidence. Let me hasten to say, however, that I do not believe it is either wise or fair to bring difficult—and particularly emotional—problems before very young children or make them feel responsible for their solution. Until the child is ready to take a part in the discussion, he should not be burdened with situations he cannot help to solve and which will only undermine his sense of security at home.

We are the sum total of all the choices we have made. There is scarcely an hour of the day in which we are not called upon to make choices of one sort or another, trivial or far-reaching. We are all beset by choices. What time shall I get up or go to bed? What shall I wear? What shall I eat? Whom shall I see? Will I take the road to the left or the one to the right?

Then come the somewhat bigger choices: What shall I do with my life? How much am I willing to give of myself, of my time, of my love? What kind of career shall I decide on—and why? That is, do I want fame, money, personal satisfaction, self-expression, or some other value?

What people will I know? This, incidentally, is a far-reaching question. All of us have had the distasteful experience of meeting the person who speaks of "knowing the right people." This reveals, of course, a lack of assurance, a tendency to judge people's value by prestige, income, or such shallow and vulgar standards. The only right people are the ones we like and value for themselves. There is a bleakness about spending hours of one's time with people with whom we can share no interests, no sense of values, no laughter.

Some of the most wonderful times of my life have been spent with people so poor that when one visited them one took one's own food to make sure there would be enough to go around. But the talk was gay and intelligent and the time spent was delightful and rewarding. Yet I have been bored to the point of pain at fantastically lavish parties. Surely I would have been stupid to spend much time with people who were not right for me.

This matter of choosing people seems of major importance to me; the narrower you make the circle of your friends, the narrower will be your experience of people and the narrower will your interests become. It is an important part of one's personal choices to decide to widen the circle of one's acquaintances whenever one can.

Then come the hard choices: What do I believe? To what extent am I ready to live up to my beliefs? How far am I ready to support them? Are there times when I lack the courage to stand up and be counted because I fear loss of prestige or popularity, of alienating my neighbors, of hurting my business or professional standing?

I am thinking particularly of prejudice as it is entering many communities where efforts are made by a few to prevent people of other races or religions from living among them. Too often, men or women who feel that this attitude is wrong will remain silent; they will not protest, they will not stand up to be counted. They are afraid of losing popularity or social prestige. They haven't the courage of their convictions, they refuse to take any responsibility for the situation.

A few years ago a couple moved into a neighborhood where the majority of the families were people of established wealth and influence. They were a friendly couple and eager to make a place for themselves, to put down roots in their new environment. But—

One evening they attended a dinner party. The conversation veered to the arrival in town of a colored preacher, who was to become the resident minister of a predominantly white congregation. Both hosts and guests were outraged by the situation and their comments grew increasingly bitter.

The couple remained silent. They wanted to be accepted, to belong, to be part of this new community. After all, no one asked their opinion. They didn't have to say anything, did they?

Well, yes, they did. They were people of integrity and courage. They exchanged glances and rose to their feet.

"We aren't angry," they said. "We like you very much.

But it makes us so unhappy to hear all this hatred that we must go."

Not unexpectedly, after a stunned silence and a period of irritation, the people who had attended the party began to feel a profound respect for the newcomers. If they did not alter any emotional prejudices, at least they were on record and their record was respected.

As I watched the Soviet training of children I was aware that, though they were called upon for obedience, there were few choices that would ever be left to them, perhaps no vital and meaningful choices. That was all done for them by the state.

In this country there is frequent criticism of the fact that, both at home and at school, our children are given too much opportunity to make their own choices and decisions, that they are given freedom before they are equipped to handle it and, therefore, they become a nuisance to themselves as well as to those around them.

I do not think that we can make an easy generalization about this. But I do think that we have not yet learned how much imposed discipline a child actually needs before he is ready for self-discipline and the acceptance of responsibility. It seems to me that a good deal of discipline in the general pattern of life can be imposed while allowing the child limited freedom. With the gradual growth of ability to accept responsibility, more and more can be required.

We have all seen one area in which there appears to be a widespread breakdown of the ability to accept responsibility: there are too many reckless drivers among young people.

They do not acknowledge responsibility for their actions when they are behind the wheel of a car. They do not feel responsible for obeying the speed laws or those about drinking and driving.

The young show-off who weaves his way in and out of traffic, puts his foot down on the accelerator as though this were a highly clever thing to do, and takes a drink before getting behind the wheel has failed to accept adult responsibility.

We cannot, of course, look to the young alone for failure to accept responsibility. We see it in the woman who waits for her husband to come home from work to pour into his tired ears her problems and leave it to him to discipline the children, to determine their actions, or even to plan what they will have for dinner!

We see it in the man who holds back from job advancement because then he will have to make the decisions and be responsible for the results. He finds it easier to sit back and let someone else take the responsibility and tell him what to do.

We see it in the inability to decide upon a career or a job, though most of one's future welfare, the core of one's life as a whole, are shaped by that decision. But here, while there is no doubt that one must make this decision, the first choice need not necessarily be the final one. There are so many unpredictable factors involved that there must be a margin for error allowed.

I am always interested when I find a youngster with the courage to change his mind in regard to his life work. This does not mean that I think it is wise for anyone to try a number of occupations or professions, hit or miss, before deciding on the one he wants. But I think if you have learned to make choices, to analyze the situation, and to use a certain amount of discipline in making yourself try a thing out so that you know whether you want it or not, you can reject it as wrong for you, while accepting the fact that you made a mistake in your first choice, and plan to do better a second time.

The temptation, too often, is to find an alibi for your first mistaken choice. "Well, the people didn't seem to be fair. . . . They were too hard on me. . . . I didn't know they would expect so much. . . ." It takes honesty and courage to accept the full responsibility when your first choice has been wrong; it takes honesty and courage to acknowledge that the fault was yours and you have no excuses to make.

It is, however, the better part of wisdom to regard the mistake as experience which will help guide you in the future, a part, though a painful part, of your education. For all of us, no matter how good our training, will make bad choices. All we can hope for is that if we are helped in youth to accept responsibility we will, through increased experience, make better choices as life goes on.

There is one point in regard to training the young to make their own choices and take responsibility for them which I feel needs some attention. Few choices are necessarily final. Nearly all choices can, on second thought, be rectified. Therefore, a child should feel that while he must decide for himself, no disaster will result if he is wrong. We must not expect of the child what we do not expect of ourselves, namely, that he will be absolutely right. We must help the child to understand that there can be no perfect choices.

The young, even those who call themselves "beat," have a touching belief in perfection. The appeal of all fairy tales, I think, lies in that sunny promise, "And so they lived happily ever after." Therefore, a choice may be a sound one and promise much, but if it does not offer perfection, the young may repent of their choice and deny it.

Just as all living is adjustment and readjustment, so all choice, to some extent, must be compromise between reality and a dream of perfection. We must try to bring the reality as close to that dream of perfection as we can, but we must not demand of it the impossible. It is only an approximation that anyone can reach, but the closer one tries to approximate it, the more he will grow. If he keeps his dream of perfection and strains toward it, he will come closer to achieving it than if he rejects the reality because it was not perfection.

Not long ago, a woman said to me, "I can't understand your optimism. I think it is hard not to be cynical when a person really looks around him."

It is impossible to be a cynic if you live a good deal with young people. Fundamentally, every young person has a feeling that the future is going to hold something of value for him. Cynicism seems to me a form of philosophical defeat. It comes only when you have given up any thought or hope of achievement.

If you care enough about certain things and work for them, I think you are bound to find them in the people you are with. To go on the theory that everything is useless before you start, that the world cannot be saved, that "you can't change human nature," in spite of the fact that we saw Hitler do it and are seeing the Soviets do it before our eyes, is a pointless business.

What matters now, as always, is not what we can't do: it is what we can and must do.

Affirmation rather than negation. It is true that I am fundamentally an optimist, that I am congenitally hopeful. I do not believe that good always conquers evil, because I have lived a long time in the world and seen that it is not true. I do not seek the pot of gold at the foot of the rainbow or think that "everything will have a happy ending" because I would like it to.

It is not wishful thinking that makes me a hopeful woman. Over and over, I have seen, under the most improbable circumstances, that man can remake himself, that he can even remake his world if he cares enough to try. And I have seen him, by the dozen, by the thousands, making that effort. Given leverage enough, a wise man said, "I could lift the world." Given incentive enough, man can remake his world. The incentive is his own well-being, the opportunity to grow to his full stature. Little by little, he is coming to know that and to grope for the point of leverage.

Surely, in the light of history, it is more intelligent to hope rather than to fear, to try rather than not to try. For one thing we know beyond all doubt: Nothing has ever been achieved by the person who says, "It can't be done."

chapter 10

How Everyone Can
Take Part in Politics

Politics is the participation of the citizen in his government.
The kind of government he has depends entirely on the quality of that participation. Therefore, every single one of us
must learn, as early as possible, to understand and accept our
duties as a citizen.

What, then, are these duties which, as citizens, we owe
our community and our government? Theodore Roosevelt
frequently declared that a man's first duty is to support himself and his family. His next is to serve his country, not only
in time of war but whenever and wherever he is needed.

The minimum, the very basic minimum, of a citizen's
duty is to cast a vote on election day. Even now, too few of us
discharge this minimal duty. By such negligence, such indifference, such sheer laziness, we discard, unused, a gift and a
privilege obtained for us at gigantic cost and sacrifice.

But if our chief obligation is to cast a vote, this carries with it a further duty—to vote intelligently. And here we hit a snag. How are you to acquire the ability to vote intelligently?

To vote intelligently you must have an understanding of issues and the different points of view as to how they can best be handled. You must have some way of appraising and evaluating the men who appeal for your suffrage to enable them to handle the issues. You must understand how things get done through political action. You must know, in general if not in particular, what kind of country you want to live in and how these issues will affect the main picture.

But how, people are constantly asking me, can one get this information? In a world so disturbed, a civilization so complicated, with an immense number of issues and many candidates for public office, how is one to know where one stands, what ideas are valid, what candidates have the qualifications to represent us adequately? These are difficult questions but they must be answered. We cannot prepare ourselves for our duties as citizens in one easy lesson. But, little by little, we can learn the rudiments and, in time, become informed and responsible voters, knowing what and whom we are voting for—and why.

It isn't easy, of course, but nothing worth while is apt to be easy. We must, for the most part, rely for much of our information on four main sources: the President of the United States, who is, or should be, the great educator of the people, bringing issues to them and explaining the situation; the great mass media of communication, newspapers, radio,

television, which are, or should be, vehicles for bringing unbiased reports of news events, economic and political conditions; the commentators who are, or should be, analysts of
the news, of economics, of contemporary history, of political
leaders, based on a wider source of information and a broader
experience than the average voter can possibly have; and discussion, frank and open, no holds barred, on men and policies with friends and neighbors.

These are the main sources of our information, the background on which our judgments are formed. They should be
adequate for the purpose. Unhappily, too often they are not.
People are constantly telling me that there are vast areas of
the country where few newspapers attempt any real cover-
age of the news. This background of information is becoming
increasingly difficult to attain. Year by year there are fewer
newspapers; it becomes more and more difficult to hear two
sides of the news.

"How are we going to find out the facts?" people ask me
over and over. "We are not afraid of forming our own judgments, but we must have a concrete and reliable body of evidence on which to base it."

Finding the facts—there's the rub. It seems to me that
the mass media do not take as seriously as they should their
immense responsibility to keep the people of the country informed. Too often, they present the news scantily and inadequately. They should present two sides of each question so
that the people can have a real opportunity to form their own
judgments. After all, both sides are news.

Of course, if one has infinite leisure or is willing to take
time from other interests, one can read widely—newspapers,
magazines, books—in an effort to get at the facts, to find
out what is actually happening, to weigh the evidence im-
partially But if there is not enough time, or the published
material is not available, people most frequently turn to the
commentators, who play an increasingly important part in
shaping the opinions of the voters.

Like the newspapers, these men vary widely in the extent
of their sources of news, in their experience and integrity in
evaluating it, in their contacts with men in high places both
in this country and abroad. Their attitude toward their function may be merely that of a gossip relating malicious stories;
or that of a propagandist for some particular point of view; or
that of an advocate for a certain type of policy; or it may be,
and fortunately is, in half a dozen cases at least, that of a man
who tries, to the best of his ability, to bring an undistorted
and unbiased account of public events to his audience. Such
men, like good newspapers, keep separate their facts and
their personal commentary.

But which ones can we rely on, people ask. This is a hard
question to answer. Indeed, there can be no definite answer.
If possible, listen to more than one and then, over a period
of weeks or even a few months, you will be able to evaluate
the facts and opinions they give you, and it may be that this
will prove one of the best ways to garner the information you
need. Most of us need some guidance in understanding the
import of events and in evaluating the various efforts that are
made to cope with them.

It is not only important but mentally invigorating to discuss political matters with people whose opinions differ radically from one's own. For the same reason, I believe it is a sound idea to attend not only the meetings of one's own party but of the opposition. Find out what people are saying, what they are thinking, what they believe. This is an invaluable check on one's own ideas. Are we right in what we think or is there a different approach that might be more effective? Are we clinging to an outmoded theory? Which policy is best for the people, best for our government, best for the world? If we are to cope intelligently with a changing world, we must be flexible and willing to relinquish opinions that no longer have any bearing on existing conditions.

By listening to and talking with a variety of people you sometimes get an entirely new slant on a question. I have often thought that I had examined a question from every side and then found that someone else could give me a completely different aspect which, in many ways, might make a difference in my opinion, however carefully I might have reasoned out my position beforehand.

Talking over political problems and theories is useful for a variety of reasons. By having to frame your ideas and beliefs in words, you are forced to crystallize, to clarify them for yourself. Through discussion you can get fresh light on situations and fresh facts about conditions. Above all, you can get the stimulation and challenge of disagreement and learn to test your beliefs and opinions, to re-examine them from a fresh viewpoint. Of course, if you merely defend your opinion without re-examination, any discussion is quite pointless.

* * *

The President of the United States is in a better position than anyone else to be the great educator of the people because he meets more people and has access to more information than anyone else. He should, by virtue of his office and his position of trust, keep the people informed about what their government is doing and make the situation clear to them. Sometimes, of course, the citizen discovers that he cannot rely on getting information from this source, even in matters that vitally concern his future and his welfare.

Not long ago, Congress was faced with the fact that, if it did nothing, our administration, under certain executive orders, would turn over nuclear knowledge to Germany and certain other countries. A few Congressmen, realizing that Congress had not been alerted to what this might mean, determined that there should be a debate. It was not fair that Congress and the public should not be aware of the power that was being given the administration.

The debate took place, but because not enough interest had been aroused nothing was accomplished. Automatically, the nuclear information was given to the countries concerned in the executive orders.

Because this decision had so wide a significance, I feel that the public should have been fully cognizant of the situation. Every time a new nation acquires this information it attains the power to take action which had been limited to the great nations who are supposed to be more responsible and aware of ways in which a third world war might start. They know this might be done literally by accident. They know, too, it might

be done by intention. As each additional nation receives nuclear information the danger is intensified and I feel the people
should be alerted and made aware of the danger.

This situation should, I think, have been brought to the
attention of the people by the President of the United States
himself, so as to give them an understanding of our foreign
policy, on which the future of all of us depends. Since, however, we cannot always rely on this, or on the alertness of the
mass media to protect our interests, I think we should require
of our representatives in Congress that they inform us more
carefully and fully than they usually do on questions which
affect our commitments with other countries and our own
destiny. For we, as responsible citizens, are inevitably responsible for what our representatives in Congress ultimately do
or fail to do.

The simplest and most obvious way in which to begin famil-
iarizing yourself with your duties as a citizen and with the
mechanics of politics is to take the trouble to pay some attention to local politics. In your own community, where the
issues are familiar to you and you are able to judge for yourself what should be done and how it should be accomplished,
there is no mystery about them. Here, too, you are generally
able to meet or at least find out about the qualifications and
personalities of the candidates, to know what their record has
been in the past, and how far it measures up to their claims
and promises.

Once you have acquired this knowledge, even on a small
local scale, you will find yourself reading and analyzing po-

litical news with more understanding. As you learn to size
up the qualities of the local candidates, you begin to be able
to project yourself farther and to come to evaluate better the
candidates on the national scene.

Here again, as in all education, the learning process
makes each step easier. As you progress from interest in local
questions to national problems and international situations,
each step deepens your interest and increases your knowledge. You will discover, to your astonishment, that within a
few years time you will have made yourself a discriminating
citizen, able to know what you have a right to expect from a
candidate, at whatever level.

Only within the last half century have people come to realize that politics is not simply a career for professionals. It is
a medium through which you, as a citizen, can accomplish
certain things for your children or your community. It is not
necessary for you to run for office. It is necessary to know how
to work through the men who represent you.

It was because of my husband's absorbed interest, many
years ago, in the mechanics of politics that I first began to
acquire a certain amount of information on the workings of
politics, and also on the uses of politics, particularly as they
affected local areas. There were, I began to realize, many
things that one could accomplish only through political action. That, I think, is a reason why a great many women become involved in politics. They are not interested primarily
in political office; they want to bring about better care of children, better schools, better health.

They discover that it is not enough to wish, however earnestly, to bring these things about. They must find out what has been done; what, specifically, must be done; they must learn what funds are available for such a purpose. Unless they have all this concrete information they find themselves at a loss when they attempt to implement their wishes. It isn't enough to say, "We need better schools." You must know what kind of schools you already have, what their shortcomings are, what has brought about this situation. You must know whether it is better buildings or better teachers you are seeking.

One of the important things for the citizen who is trying to understand politics is to study human nature. Politicians are neither all bad nor all good. They vary like all human beings. Often a citizen endeavoring to accomplish a certain thing for his community will find that he cannot do it simply because of the personalities involved. A man in business must learn to understand the men with whom he works and to vary his methods to suit an individual with special characteristics, always aware that what is accomplished will depend on his ability to persuade the individual that he believes the thing should be done. So the citizen dealing with politicians may find that he has to try a dozen different methods in handling a dozen different people. It is the person who learns best how to do this who has discovered the secret of leadership.

While it is usually unnecessary to run for political office oneself to accomplish results through political action, there are times when it proves to be more effective. As an instance, in a small town in Virginia the women could not persuade the existing town administration to pick up the garbage or to provide adequate and safe street lighting. They rose up and elected an entire woman's administration, set the situation right, and, next election, returned to their private lives.

I have no desire to run for any office. Rather than hold office myself I prefer to work through my own elected representatives. Frequently, of course, one fails to get what one wants, or at best one has to accept a compromise. But it is an extraordinarily interesting thing to get things done; to find that, as a result of a certain amount of work, not only digging out facts but getting other people to work with one, something has been accomplished.

Digging out the facts. This comes down largely to seeing what you look at and understanding what you see. Many years ago, my husband taught me how to observe conditions, what to look for. This is not as easy as it sounds and it requires considerable groundwork. If—as I often did when I was trying to assemble information for my husband—one visits hospitals or prisons to find out how they are managed, one must know what constitutes a good hospital or a good prison. One must have some yardstick by which to evaluate them.

I discovered my yardstick in the state of New York because that was where my education began. I remember going into one hospital for the mentally ill. I really thought I had inspected it thoroughly.

My husband was waiting in the car when I came out. I made my report. "Was it overcrowded?" he asked me.

I didn't have the faintest idea.

He became specific. "Were there beds in the corridors?"

Yes, there had been.

"Did you look in the closets off the wards? Were any beds stacked there?"

It had not occurred to me to look there.

"How close together were the beds in the wards?" I looked at him blankly. "Is there access to each bed or do the patients have to climb over another bed to get to their own?"

I shook my head. I hadn't noticed because I hadn't even thought of checking on that.

"What is the food like?" Franklin went on with his relentless questions.

I was cheered; I knew all about that. "I went over the menus for the week. They are very good."

"But what," he wanted to know, "was in the kettles on the stove?"

After that, I knew what to look for. Whether in an institution or a CCC camp, I did not stop with the menus. I looked into every pot on the stove. How often newsmen would ask me why on earth I looked into all the kettles. But I had learned my lesson. At least I thought so—until the King of England came to visit in Washington.

He asked to visit a CCC camp and I followed along. Here, I discovered, was a trained inspector. From his youth he had been drilled, trained painstakingly to know what to look for. When he was told that the boys had made the furniture in the dining room he had the tables turned upside down so he could see how they were put together. He looked at all the supplies and at everything on the stove.

In the dormitories he felt the mattresses. He asked to see

the work shoes provided for the boys. He examined the quality of the blankets. Never before had I realized the training of a constitutional monarch.

That was one of those swelteringly hot days in Washington. The boys were drawn up in two lines. The King and Queen walked past the boys. He spoke to every alternate boy, asking him whether he liked the camp or whether he thought it would help him in the future or whether he knew of a better alternative. The Queen spoke to each boy whom the King had passed by.

Later in the afternoon my husband told me that part of my duty would be to present to the King the heads of various government agencies at a tea party at the White House and to explain their duties. I couldn't possibly, I thought with a sinking heart, recall all their names, remember the particular duties of each. But as I presented each man and before I could explain his duties, the King would say, "Oh, yes, Mr. So-and-so, your position is . . . and your work is . . ."

That night at dinner I asked the King how on earth he had been able to identify all those people and relate them to their jobs.

"But that," he said, "was only part of the briefing I had before I started this morning."

I knew then something of the training and discipline that went into making a good King. And I remembered, too, how the head of the CCC camp, looking across the fields baking under a burning sun, had said, "It is a terribly hot walk across the fields. The boys prepared their quarters for your inspection but they will understand if you do not go."

And the King answered promptly, "If they expected us, we will go."

Having acquired training in getting at facts and evaluating them while my husband was Governor of New York, I found this preliminary training invaluable when he went to Washington in evaluating the new projects which were constantly being brought up at that time. For instance, they were trying out, under Sanford Bates, remarkable head of the prison system, camps for prisoners before their release, to accustom them to more freedom and teach them some kind of trade.

This seemed to me a good thing, particularly with youthful offenders who might return to prison a second time because they had gone out, unskilled and unprepared to meet a harsh world, which did not want to take a chance on giving work to someone who had been in prison.

My going about the country and inspecting institutions and new experiments which were being tried out to meet various situations would have been valueless unless I had been able to look for something that others did not. Other inspectors could discover whether a project was efficient, whether the work was good, whether the employees were needed in their jobs. What I looked for, as a rule, was to find out the effect of the project on individual cases. Did it provide them with more security in looking for work in the future? Were they learning a skill or regaining self-respect and confidence? One of the difficulties in the first years of my husband's administration was that many people had lost confidence in the ability of their government to function so as to make life possible for them.

What it came down to was the unspoken question: Can democracy meet our human everyday needs? So it was a tremendously important thing to have the feeling that the country was coming back and could indeed meet their needs. I tried to get at the human values that were being restored and what this meant to the strength of the country as a whole.

Whether this painfully amassed information was of any value to my husband I don't know. But it was invaluable to me later when I came to travel through the world. It helped enormously in understanding people who were living at a bare subsistence level, in evaluating what they felt and thought, in grasping what stresses they would be under when it came to rehabilitating or developing their own country.

Getting at the facts. Learning to see for ourselves what our institutions are and how they function. This is a part of the duty of a citizen.

As we become better citizens and learn to accept personal responsibility for the actions of our representatives, we can have a prodigious effect upon what they do. The man in politics who has a passive or apathetic constituency, who does not know what they think or feel or want, who receives no response in the form of a word of approbation for a good action or of condemnation for a bad one, has little incentive to try to become better and more forceful on his job.

The average practical politician, whether in the smallest local job or at the higher levels, is subjected to almost ceaseless pressures of one kind and another. It takes strength and honor and conviction to stand firm against them. If he has no support from his constituency he has little incentive to make the fight.

Thomas Jefferson said that individual responsibility for the well-being of the community as a whole was an absolutely necessary ingredient to success in a democracy. Democracy, he pointed out—not being a man to turn away from the unpleasant when it was necessary for people to know the truth—is the most difficult type of government simply because it requires this kind of responsibility.

Because it is the most highly developed type of government, democracy requires the most highly developed citizens. Whether we, as a whole, are willing to accept this responsibility and live up to it is something of which I cannot be sure. But we cannot be reminded too often that each of us is responsible for our attitude and our way of life, because they will in turn affect our government.

Once again, I think we must learn our duties as citizens, as we learn most of our basic values, at home. It is easy to make children insular, intolerant, and apathetic about the course of events. It is almost as easy to make them informed, interested, and responsible citizens.

At one time I attended a Rotary Club luncheon where the speakers were high-school children who had taken part in a model assembly, each child serving as the representative of a different country. The Rotary Club had sponsored the children from a particular high school in this locality and the children were at the Rotary Club luncheon to report on what they had done.

A teen-age girl got up and said, "I represent Ghana. Few of you have ever heard the name of my country, but it is important because it is one of the first in Africa to obtain self-government from colonial rule."

Speaking simply and clearly, she discussed Ghana's economy, its efforts to form a government, and the problems it had encountered. I watched, fascinated, as this child brought her facts to an older group, quite evidently ahead of their thinking on many points, and in some cases even ahead of their ability to understand.

The result of this experiment was that the following year the youngsters were eager to have another model assembly and to learn about more countries. At the same time, they had become interested in politics as history, imbued with a sense of their own responsibility toward the functioning of their country.

Some months ago, when I was visiting an uncle of mine in Florida, a few of the local politicians came to call on me, though we do not as a rule see eye to eye on many problems.

"Well, Mrs. Roosevelt," one of them said, "you ought to be satisfied. We'll end by having integration. Our children do not see it our way. My little boy asked me last autumn what all the fuss was about. He did not mind sitting by Johnny in school. Johnny is the little colored boy who plays with him."

One of the other men said, "My little girl came to me and said, 'I don't see what you are all talking about. Susie and I get on at school as well as we do at home.'"

My response was, "I am very glad to hear this and if you will let them alone, they will be all right."

Unless indoctrinated, a child is too logical to understand discrimination. It is the duty of every self-respecting citizen to oppose the prejudiced indoctrination of children, to take his courage in his hands and say clearly, "I do not agree with this. I feel we are performing a great and senseless injustice."

But the courage to go against a sweep of feeling, to be an awkward minority, to stand up and be counted, even when it makes one unpopular, is not as prevalent as it should be. We have a long way to go to achieve responsible citizenship and common self-respecting humanity.

An interesting experiment has been made to prepare young people from all parts of our country for more responsible citizenship. This is the Encampment for Citizenship, a group sponsored by the Ethical Culture Society. It now has one camp in summer on the outskirts of New York City and another on the campus of Berkeley University.

Regardless of race, creed, or color, these young people spend six weeks working, learning, and playing together. They come out with a deepened understanding of the workings of democracy. The fact that, later on, the percentage who cast a vote is far higher than the average shows that they have actually been imbued with a real sense of their responsibility as citizens.

Given half a chance, the young, I think, can be trusted not only to accept political responsibility but to welcome it, for with each effort to shoulder a burden comes strength, and with strength comes confidence. With confidence enough, a nation is invincible. No man is defeated without until he has first been defeated within.

Actually, it is difficult not to be swept into the life of the community in which we belong, not to play some part, however small, in what happens to it. Each such participation is healthy not only for the citizen but for his community.

One of the local organizations which is, I think, most heartening to see in action is the volunteer fire department in many small communities. These are young men from all walks of life who, in time of emergency, work together to save life and property. Anyone who has ever seen a volunteer fire department go into action, seen people of all kinds and sorts and conditions drop whatever they were doing and join the battle against fire, the common enemy, has a sense of the essential wholeness and unity of community life that is rarely as intense under other circumstances.

Not long ago, there was an account of a group of volunteer firemen who risked their lives to save the inmates of a prison, where they were trapped by fire. They were not concerned with the men's crimes, they were concerned only with saving human beings who were in peril. Many of them were injured but the work went on.

The public was left with a deep feeling of pride for these men and a deep shame that they themselves had been too indolent to know the conditions of their own prisons.

Often, when I make points like these to a somewhat torpid group I will meet with the response, "Oh, I can't conceive of having anything to do with politics. Think of the corruption. He who touches tar, etc. . . ."

Corruption? Well, unhappily, yes. There is corruption

in politics because there are human beings in politics. There is corruption in business and in law and in medicine. But when there is corruption it is because we allow it to grow and flourish.

There is only one way of combating corruption: that is not by eschewing politics; it is by developing standards of honor, living up to them, and requiring them of our candidates. Let's take that bugbear of politics, bribery. Today, there is a growing tendency, and a most healthy one, to regard the person who offers the bribe as equally guilty with the person who takes the bribe. This attitude of equal disgrace and punishment for both will go far to eliminate the ugliness of bribery.

There have to be two sides of corruption. The man who seeks the woman on the streets should be held as responsible as the woman. The man who buys dope is as guilty as the peddler who sells it. The speeder who bribes the policeman is responsible for corruption in the police department and the breakdown of law enforcement.

Not long ago, a police commissioner lamented to me that he was frequently unable to bring transgressors in his department to book because, when the time came, the public refused to testify against them. If the public itself condones or fosters corruption there is not a great deal that can be done about it higher up.

In a very undramatic way, people can do much to prevent corruption in politics, as in other areas of life. They must have the courage to live up to their own principles, to stand firmly by what they believe. This is often a painfully difficult thing to do. It requires unrelenting discipline and unshaken faith in certain values.

The person who drives at seventy-five miles an hour in a forty-mile zone regards it as a trivial matter, but the law was made for the public safety, and when he breaks that law, he is undermining the fabric on which our whole society rests—the due process of law.

Sometimes I think that the fact that, in early days, we administered the law ourselves may have affected our present attitude toward obeying the law. At that time, there was no recognized force of law to keep the peace. The situation is different today and yet too many people still live as though they were in a frontier town where they can take the law into their own hands as they see fit.

One thing no one can dispute: If you want a world ruled by law and not by force you must build up, from the very grassroots, a respect for law. It is the code we have created for our mutual safety and well-being. It is our bulwark against chaos. It is the fabric of our civilization. We cannot rip the fabric nor weaken it without danger to the whole institution which we call government. For the chief duty of the citizen is to make his government the best possible medium for the peaceful and prosperous conduct of life.

chapter 11

Learning to Be a Public Servant

For some forty years, more or less, I have, willy-nilly, been thrust into the curious and exciting world of politics, talked with public servants on every level, been plunged into political activities that ranged from house-to-house canvassing on a local scale to observing the making of policy on the highest level.

What have I learned from it that might be of value to a person who is preparing himself to become a public servant?

First of all, let me say that few people have ever deliberately prepared themselves to become public servants. Startling as the idea may appear, it is perfectly natural, because so few people begin their careers by planning to run for political office. There are several main reasons for this: first, of course, politics provides at best an uncertain future, with one's position at stake every few years. Second, it affords less financial reward than falls to the lot of able and competent men in almost any other field of endeavor.

So the men on whose shoulders we place the heavy burden of running a great government, of keeping it economically sound, of maintaining the delicate balance of peace in the world, of looking after the welfare of the people in the most effective way, have usually entered politics more or less accidentally, or so late in life that their ideas may tend to be fixed.

There are certain fundamental things that any man deciding to become a public servant must face.

First of all, if you are going to run for elective office, you must be sure either that you have earned enough money in a previous job or that you have enough connections so that you may return to active work in your community if you are voted out of office. Otherwise, if you are completely dependent for your livelihood on your salary from elective office, you will find it terribly difficult to avoid being forced into compromises out of fear of not being re-elected. It is an unhappy truth that a man entirely dependent on his salary as a public servant is dangerously vulnerable. He is afraid to take risks. He is afraid to do an unpopular thing, even though he may be convinced that it is right. He is sometimes open to deals.

Second, the man planning to take public office must be sure that his family is willing to accept this mode of life, which in many respects is unlike any other. The family must be willing to accept the fact that they will live in glass houses; they must be willing to forgo a larger income. My husband used to say that anyone connected with a man or woman in public office needed the hide of a rhinoceros.

Third, the man must have a genuine love of people and a deep desire to achieve something which can be accomplished only through public service. He must have a sense of satisfaction in doing something for his country. This, I think, is almost essential if public service is to have any validity. A politician interested only in his own personal advancement is not only useless as a public servant but he will eventually fail. The basic success of any politician lies in his ability to make his own interests those of his constituents, so that he merges into the community which he serves. Then and then only can he accomplish what he wishes to do.

A congressman or a senator will discover that the term "public servant" is an elastic one in the minds of his constituents, when they remember him at all. He will be asked to perform the most trivial errands. The Department of Agriculture is supposed to have developed a new kind of seed. Will he please let the voter know about it right away? He will be asked for information about points of law affecting business in his area. His ability and his worth to his constituents may be judged solely by the number of public works and buildings he manages to get allotted to his state.

He is expected to get tickets for his constituents so they can see the White House or sit in the gallery of Congress to listen to debates. He is expected to be available to shake hands with the voters when they come to Washington, and chat with them for a while.

At the same time he must be at hand on the floor and in

committee rooms and in his office. He should endeavor to get across to his constituents the fact that, as their representative, he has an obligation to think not only of their interests but of how the things they want will fit into the economy of the country as a whole or what is happening in some other section of the country. The public servant who wants to stick by his guns will find it a great comfort to realize that he does not *need* to be re-elected to office in order to earn his living and support his family.

In the past, it was difficult to find public servants who were able to take a national rather than a local view of conditions. One of my favorite anecdotes about Theodore Roosevelt concerns an observation he made one day when, as President, he was pacing the floor.

"I wish," he broke out characteristically, "that for just ten minutes I could be President and Congress too."

When he was asked why he replied, "I would pass a law that every congressman must visit at least two-thirds of the states before he comes to Washington."

Today, we not only expect our politicians to have a national concept but an international concept. In fact, it is essential that they have it. Of course, we cannot expect them to know the world as a whole, but soon after they reach Washington, they have an opportunity to see much of the world. *How* they see and what they get from these trips is all-important. Sometimes, unfortunately, it is sheer waste, but sometimes new vistas open up which transform commonplace, narrow individuals into really good public servants.

*   *   *

Ideally, a politician should be a statesman. He must understand the people of the area where he is working. He must
know their needs and their desires. He must be able to represent them in the work he has undertaken, whether as governor, congressman, or whatever. He must master the details
that affect the job, because it is the sum total of these details
which will mean the sum total of his success or failure with
the people whom he serves.

He must have an over-all interest in the big questions
that touch his community and an understanding of how
these questions in turn are affected by the broader national
and international questions, and have the ability to bring the
whole picture back to the people of his community, so en-
abling them to become a part of the world community.

It is a valuable asset to a politician if he has a sense of
what is usually called timing, which means recognizing the
appropriate time for doing certain things, the moment at
which people and circumstances are ripe to achieve results.

Perhaps an important ingredient in timing is patience,
an enormous amount of patience. A second ingredient in timing is a clear awareness of the extent to which the people are
with you. A leader must not get too far ahead or he will out-
distance his followers; but he must move at least a step ahead.
He must take his people with him. I have occasionally seen
my husband make grave mistakes by wrong timing, moving
ahead before the people were ready for the next step, but he
made few such mistakes.

An important ingredient for the politician is the ability
to attract and draw people to him. All political action is fil-

tered through other human beings. Any man entering political life should make it a rule never to miss an opportunity
to meet people, to learn new things, to widen and deepen his
experience. He must learn to cultivate a sympathetic understanding of what is going on in another person's mind, or he
risks offending when he least intends to do so.

This quality is important in one's personal relationships,
important in business, and vitally important in politics,
particularly in international affairs, where we are dealing
with all kinds and varieties of people and differences of background and custom. Unless we can project ourselves into the
minds of others, we are in danger of creating differences between us, for we will not be able to make them see what our
motives are or what we are attempting to achieve until we
know how they feel and can build a bridge of understanding
with them through communication that is unclouded.

I have been talking as though men were the only crea-
tures to enter politics, but women are doing so increasingly,
particularly in their own communities. They have some advantages and some disadvantages. They will generally find
that men will tend to "keep them in their place." They are
not apt to be in on vital decisions. They have to be alert to
see they are not kept from attending important meetings.
Sometimes they have to be extremely insistent if they are to
succeed in carrying the full responsibility of the job to which
they have been appointed or elected.

The only real drawback of women in politics that I have
noticed is that they are more sensitive to criticism than men.
They are slower to learn that they must stick to what they

think is right, whether it is popular or not. The newspapers may belabor you on Monday, but by Friday they and the public have forgotten all about the matter. The sensible thing is for the recipient of the criticism to forget it too.

In the not-too-distant past, when we lived in a stable, unchanging world, there was room in political life for men whose opinions had crystallized. They could perform reliable and useful service. But today we live in a world in a state of flux, of shifting balance of power, of shifting alliances, of changing economics, of science transforming life and threatening to extinguish it. The problems are new.

During the past twenty years we have actually accomplished a revolution in this country, without having been conscious that we had one. It did not have the elements of the usual violent upheaval of people in protest; it came about largely through the acceptance, when we had a period of great economic stress in the thirties, of the fact that government had a responsibility for its people. Our type of capitalism went through drastic alterations, with a complete change in the thinking of the people, and a new concept of the function and duties of government for the welfare of the people.

To meet these new challenges we look for new ingredients in our public servants, an elasticity and flexibility of mind that enables them to change in order to meet changes; an alert and hospitable intelligence that can grasp new issues, new conditions, new peoples. We look especially for a man who knows what he thinks and can make his views clearly understood without ambiguity or hedging. We need a man with the courage to stand up and be counted on major issues.

It is no longer possible for us to look back over our shoulders if we are to keep abreast of our world, let alone maintain leadership. We cannot say, "Nothing has changed," or "The old ways were best." The point is that the old conditions are gone and we are left confronting the new.

This is not our dilemma alone. It is a world dilemma. Everywhere alert leaders are trying to meet it intelligently. India is still regarded as one of the most backward countries, but India has made one of the most revolutionary changes of all: legally abolished the caste system. Now, of course, prejudice and long-instilled custom move less quickly than the law, so that caste still exists in actuality. However, little by little, step by step, the change grows, the new idea takes hold, is implemented, becomes fact.

If India can tackle a problem on which its social, religious, economic, and political life has been based for centuries, surely it is possible to find public servants in the United States who are willing to grapple with new conditions in new ways. For in our relationship with all the peoples of the world we must recognize and accept new conditions.

Many problems that once seemed to us of domestic importance only now have international importance. This is particularly true of the problems affecting our minorities. These now have a vital bearing on our relations with other peoples in the world. The greater number of the people now gaining freedom in Asia and Africa are of colored blood. They seek equality, freedom, and justice. They want to be regarded as equals. If we attempt to maintain two classes of citizens in this country they will distrust our attitude toward them.

It is essential that the public servant be willing to learn all he can about people everywhere. We can no longer afford to be ignorant. On ignorance of a people or a situation a whole mistaken policy can be established.

This struck me most when I had a long conversation several years ago with Mr. Khrushchev. No matter how much I argued, no matter how many facts I marshaled to enforce my opinion, I could not convince him that the workers in the United States were not only better off but really happier than those in Russia. He had been taught that the "capitalistic slaves" were unhappy. They waited only for a chance to throw off their chains.

"Look at your strikes," he told me. "They are proof that the men are desperate."

"Desperate men don't strike," I replied. "During the depression there were few strikes. A strike is a sign of a worker's faith that he can better his condition."

Mr. Khrushchev was not convinced. He had always believed in the theory of the hopeless "capitalistic slaves." Much of his views of the Western world, much of his policy, much of his picture of the future was predicated on it.

Then he came to visit the United States, to see for himself, to talk to the farmers, the industrial workers, the labor leaders. Today Mr. Khrushchev knows something about the American workers. It is bound to affect his point of view about the probability of world revolution.

*   *   *

The mechanics of politics vary in different places, but if you want to start work with your party it is well to become a local committee member, then a county and then a state committee member. You can, as a reward for your work, be made a delegate to the state or national conventions, and in these capacities you will meet and know people and learn to understand how they function.

Sometimes you are bound to find politics an unsavory business. Many people involved in it have only personal interests and seek to gain personal advantages by any available means. Perhaps one of the important things to learn is how pressures are brought to bear on people in public office.

Bribery is not solely a matter of money, of expenses paid for favors received. It can take many forms. It may be an implied promise of higher office or greater influence. In my early days in Albany I discovered why the Irish are such good politicians. Big Tim Sullivan would pass around in front of a colleague's desk and stop to say, "You're going to vote for So-and-so's bill, aren't you? He's your friend, you know. We must vote for our friends."

It seemed incredible to him that one would not vote for a friend. Whether the bill was bad or good was never mentioned. The important thing was that one's friend was backing it.

Occasionally in the United Nations, when the United States had made up its mind on a policy, I would hear some brash young political adviser say, "I think we can get such and such votes. We'll twist their arms a little." This meant no open threat, just a suggestion that if one didn't back one's

friends something might happen. It was all done most diplo-
matically and the top people, of course, were never supposed
to know of these activities.

There are countless other methods of applying pressure,
and if you are elected to office, you will see them for yourself.

Bribery seems always to be with us. It is accepted currently
with cynicism because it is regarded as general practice. Now
and then, public apathy is jolted to awareness of the moral
issues involved; their collective disapproval and the force of
public opinion change the situation for the better. The recent
television quiz scandal revealed a general, a widespread frame
of mind: "Oh, well, everyone does it, you know."

What "everyone" did seemed all right until it met the
fierce white light of publicity. Then the collective conscience
of the public was aroused and there was a re-examination
of moral issues. How much, people wondered uneasily, were
they as individuals to blame for this widespread dishonesty?
How much of it grew out of accepting as truth what they
knew was not true?

Politics can be dirty business when it operates on a low
level. It can also be a profoundly stimulating business, when
the appeal is to the best in human nature. It is, like all areas
of human activity and experience, what we choose to make it.

Each man who decides to become a public servant will,
sooner or later, or, perhaps, over and over, be confronted by a
basic question which only he can answer: How much are you
willing to compromise?

Now one thing is sure. To some extent, he will have to
compromise. He can never achieve his ideal. He must advance

step by step. But he must always keep sharply before his eyes his main objectives. If he abandons them, he becomes a mere opportunist.

Often a man will have to face a choice: Will you stand firmly for a certain principle and risk defeat, or will you compromise on the issue so you will not be defeated and will still have an opportunity to accomplish other things?

The problems of the public servant are many: his future is always uncertain; his pay is relatively low; he is faced with an infinite number of perplexities; he has to meet and cope with serious problems; he is constantly bombarded with pressures for favors, for basic compromises; he is offered bribery on every level from openly offered gifts to hidden benefits.

In return for this he often meets with indifference from his constituency, or with quite unreasonable demands. He is regarded by many not as a public servant to be honored but as fit game for scoffing, for every conceivable discourtesy.

A good public servant becomes so at a high cost of personal sacrifice. We need such men; when we find them we owe them our gratitude and, above all, our respect.

Afterword

Having come to the end of the book I am filled with misgivings. As far as possible I have tried to answer, for myself as well as for others, the question: What have you learned by living? One is in danger of sounding dogmatic, as though one had found all the answers, which would be nonsense; or of sounding infallible, as though one had made no mistakes, which would be equally absurd.

Looking back over these pages I thought in chagrin, "But there is really nothing new here. I have discovered no fresh wisdom." Then I remembered my favorite passage in Norman Douglas's *South Wind*, in which the elderly Count attempts to pass on to the young Denis such wisdom as he has learned. I would like to quote it here:

"What did he say?" asked Denis.

"The old teacher? Let me see . . . He said: do not be discomposed by the opinions of inept persons. Do not swim with the crowd. They who are all things to their neighbors, cease to be anything to themselves. Even a diamond can have too many facets. Avoid the attrition of vulgar minds; keep your edges intact. He also said: A man can protect himself with fists or

sword but his best weapon is his intellect. A weapon must be
forged in the fire. The fire, in our case, is tribulation. It must
also be kept untarnished. If the mind is clean, the body can
take care of itself. He said: delve deeply; not too deeply into the
past, for it may make you derivative; nor yet into yourself—it
will make you introspective. Delve into the living world and
strive to bind yourself to its movement by a chain of your own
welding. Once that contact is established, you are unassailable.
Externalize yourself! He told me many things of this kind. You
think I was consoled by his words? Not in the slightest degree.
I was annoyed. It struck me, at the moment, as quite ordinary
advice. In fact, I thought him rather a hypocrite; anyone could
have spoken as he did! I was so disappointed that I went to
him next day and told him frankly what I thought of his counsel. He said—do you know what he said?"

"I cannot even guess."

"He said: 'What is all wisdom save a collection of plati-
tudes? Take fifty of our current proverbial sayings—they are
so trite, so threadbare, that we can hardly bring our lips to
utter them. None the less they embody the concentrated experience of the race, and the man who orders his life according
to their teaching cannot go far wrong. How easy that seems!
Has any one ever done so? Never. Has any man ever attained
to inner harmony by pondering the experience of others? Not
since the world began! He must pass through the fire.'"

"I had no teacher like that," observed Denis. "He must
have been a man of the right kind."

"Oh, he meant well, the old rascal," replied the Count
with a curious little smile.

About the Author

ELEANOR ROOSEVELT revolutionized the role of First Lady during her tenure from 1933 to 1945. In the years following, she served as a delegate to the United Nations General Assembly, where she chaired both the Human Rights Commission and the Commission on the Status of Women and helped draft the Universal Declaration of Human Rights. She was the author of several books, and she died on November 7, 1962.

COOL PAPERBACKS, COOL PRICE

How to Be a Woman	*You Learn by Living*	*Profiles in Courage*	*The Orchardist*
Caitlin Moran	Eleanor Roosevelt	John F. Kennedy	Amanda Coplin

OLIVE EDITIONS for $10 EACH

Available for a Limited Time Only

The Space Between Us	*So Big*	*Pilgrim at Tinker Creek*	*The Professor and the Madman*
Thrity Umrigar	Edna Ferber	Annie Dillard	Simon Winchester